英美经典影视与文化教程
Anglo-American Classic Movies and Culture

主 编 孙建光 王春梅

·南京·

内容提要

本书以历史、信仰、名人、节日、教育、皇室、传奇及文学经典等为主线，选取了经典的电影，在介绍了这些影片的背景知识和故事情节的基础之上，通过设置的社会、历史、文化等板块帮助学习者在欣赏影片、提升语言能力的同时拓展知识面，培养思辨能力，树立符合国情和责任担当的价值观。

图书在版编目(CIP)数据

英美经典影视与文化教程 / 孙建光,王春梅主编. — 南京：东南大学出版社,2018.6(2021.3 重印)
ISBN 978-7-5641-7707-2

Ⅰ.①英… Ⅱ.①孙… ②王… Ⅲ.①英语-阅读教学-高等学校-教材 ②影视艺术-鉴赏-世界 Ⅳ.①H319.4:J

中国版本图书馆 CIP 数据核字(2018)第 069260 号

英美经典影视与文化教程　Yingmei Jingdian Yingshi Yu Wenhua Jiao cheng

主　编	孙建光　王春梅	责任编辑	刘　坚	
电　话	(025)83793329　QQ:635353748	电子邮件	liu-jian@seu.edu.cn	
出版发行	东南大学出版社	出 版 人	江建中	
地　址	南京市四牌楼2号	邮　编	210096	
销售电话	(025)83794561/83794174/83794121/83795801/83792174　83795802/57711295(传真)			
网　址	http://www.seupress.com	电子邮件	press@seupress.com	
经　销	全国各地新华书店	印　刷	广东虎彩云印刷有限公司	
开　本	787mm×1092mm　1/16	印　张	11.5	
字　数	300千字			
版　次	2018年6月第1版	印　次	2021年3月第2次印刷	
书　号	ISBN 978-7-5641-7707-2			
定　价	48.00元			

* 未经许可,本书内文字不得以任何方式转载、演绎,违者必究。
* 东大版图书如有印装错误,可直接向营销部调换,电话:025-83791830。

前言
PREFACE

　　欣赏英文电影是大学生学习英文、了解英美国家社会文化的一个重要手段,然而,很多大学生欣赏英文影片仅满足于视觉享受和情节观赏,忽略了影片本身所体现的社会文化价值以及影片对白中的语言价值。编者在大学开设"英美影视与文化"课程多年,其间一直积极思考与探索如何才能更充分地发掘英文影片的教学价值,因而完成了本教程的编写。希望本教程既能为大学生观赏电影提供新的视角,也能在一定程度上提高他们的英文水平和对英美国家社会文化的认知。

　　《英美经典影视与文化教程》突破了传统的影视欣赏较为单一的层面,聚焦于影视中的文化因素,使得学生通过影视欣赏,了解西方人的语言思维、文化思维,既能模仿地道的英语表达,又能了解西方人的文化思维及文化知识,实现英语教育模式的立体化。

　　本教程共分八个单元,涵盖了历史、信仰、名人、节日、教育、皇室、传奇及文学经典等西方文化的主要领域:第一单元以历史为主线,让学生了解英格兰历史、美国独立战争史和第二次世界大战的相关历史知识。通过影视欣赏,学生能够对英格兰和美利坚民族的创国史有深刻的认识,同时能深入思考战争的残酷性,激励青年学生树立起爱国情怀,捍卫来之不易的当代和平生活。第二单元以宗教为主线,介绍了英国和美国的主要宗教派别,并对各教派之间的联系与区别有一种直观的认识。同时还选取了圣经故事、诺亚方舟的故事,教育人类要具有爱心、善心。第三单元以名人为主线,选取了具有代表性的人物。撒切尔夫人是英国历史上第一位女首相,创造了蝉联三届、也是自19世纪初利物浦伯爵以来连任时间最长的英国首相。她是英国历史上最优秀的首相之一。亚伯拉罕·林肯任总统期间,美国爆发内战,史称"南北战争"。林肯坚决反对国家分裂,他废除了奴隶制度,颁布了《宅地法》《解放黑人奴隶宣言》。林肯击败了南方分离势力,维护了美利坚联邦的统一。内战结束后不久,作为首位共和党总统的林肯遇刺身亡。他是第一位遭遇刺杀的美国总统,多次被评为美国历史上最伟大的总统。马克·艾略特·扎克伯格,社交网站Facebook(脸书)的创始人兼首席执行官,被人们冠以"第二盖茨"的美誉,曾是全球最年轻的自行创业亿万富豪。这些人物具有典型性,或是为国家发展,或是维护国家统一,或是青年创业精英等,具有满满的正能量。第四单元以西方假日为主线,重点选取了圣诞节前夕暖人的爱情故事、土拨鼠日和复活节等故事或人物,以凸显大爱和邪恶与抗争等主旋律,培养学生的博爱之心及勇于和邪恶势力作斗争的勇气。

第五单元以教育为主线,让学生了解美国与英国教育现状、体系及改革相关知识,使学生能结合我国教育现状进行思辨性分析比较。第六单元以英国皇室生活为主线,让学生了解英国的皇室生活、主要代表性人物,对英国的君主立宪制能有比较深刻的理解,同时可以思考为什么该制度在我国无法实行,增强学生对我国社会主义制度优越性的认同感。第七单元以传奇故事为主线,介绍了英美国家传奇人物的伟大英雄形象或采用后现代的解构主义思想,描写小人物的非常规的行为,引导学生树立正确的价值观。第八单元以文学作品为主线,选取了由文学作品改编而来的影视,让学生从读字视角和读图视角来审视文学作品中的人物刻画、情景再现,拓展学生对文学作品的认知度。

  本教程选材经典,窥探到人生、命运、友谊、爱情、传统、道德、死亡、迷惘、教育等人性和心灵的诸多方面。每部影片都分别介绍了背景知识和故事情节,收录了多段精彩对白,辅以语言文化注释和理解问答,帮助读者体会近似真实生活场景的英语,解答学习者在看、听英语电影过程中遇到的典型问题和困惑,使学习者能流畅地看电影或听录音,每单元还附有影评,学习者可以通过影评,提高其赏析能力,加深对影片内容及其所反映的社会、历史、文化背景的理解和领悟。课后练习设计契合学生的欣赏需求,同时注重提高学生的语言应用能力。

  本教程的特色是按照主题编排章节,每个单元三部影片,第一部和第二部影片可供课堂教学,第三部影片可作为自学材料,供同学们进一步拓展使用;除了第六单元外每个单元都包括英美两国的相关影片,有助于读者增进对该类型影片及相关文化的了解。本教程所选影片既有经典的如《乱世佳人》,也有兼具时代性和观赏性的好莱坞大片如《珍珠港》《七宗罪》等。教程全英文写作,对较难的词汇给出了汉语解释;每一单元既提供了影片的基本介绍与相关的文学链接,也提供了配套的练习。本教程既可以作为高等院校大学英语课程的后续拓展课程,也可以作为公共选修课程教材,同时也适合对英文电影及西方文化感兴趣的读者用作参考读物。

  本教程由孙建光教授策划统筹,由孙建光、王春梅主编,多位教师参编,具体编写分工如下:周晗负责第一、二单元,王春梅负责第三、四、五、六单元,李利红和王颖璇分别负责第七、第八单元,孙建光负责全书的审订工作。本书在编写过程中得到了朱建新教授、左进教授、张强华教授的大力支持,同时得到了英国学者 Shelley Thomson 的帮助,在此表示衷心感谢。感谢东南大学出版社编审刘坚博士后所提供的大量支持与帮助。本书在编写过程中参考了国内外著作以及网络上的相关内容,由于选材广泛,在主要参考书目处如有疏漏还望谅解,并向相关的作者谨表谢意。由于编者水平有限,难免挂一漏万,书中不足之处肯请使用本教程的教师和同学批评指正。此外,本教程还制作了配套的课件,如果有教学需要,请邮件联系 daisywang1977@126.com。

编者
2017 年 12 月

目录
CONTENTS

Unit One　History

Section A　Braveheart / 2
Section B　The Patriot / 11
Section C　Pearl Harbor / 18

Unit Two　Religion

Section A　Brideshead Revisited / 24
Section B　Se7en / 34
Section C　Noah / 39

Unit Three　Celebrities

Section A　The Iron Lady / 44
Section B　Lincoln / 56
Section C　The Social Network / 63

Unit Four　Holidays

Section A　Love Actually / 68
Section B　Groundhog Day / 76
Section C　Rise of the Guardians / 83

Unit Five　Education

　　　　Section A　Dead Poets Society / 89
　　　　Section B　The History Boys / 100
　　　　Section C　Accepted / 105

Unit Six　British Royalty

　　　　Section A　The Queen / 110
　　　　Section B　The King's Speech / 119
　　　　Section C　Henry VIII (2003) / 125

Unit Seven　Legends

　　　　Section A　King Arthur / 131
　　　　Section B　Robin Hood, the Prince of Thieves / 141
　　　　Section C　The Pursuit of D. B. Cooper / 148

Unit Eight　Literature

　　　　Section A　Pride and Prejudice / 155
　　　　Section B　Gone with the Wind / 164
　　　　Section C　For Whom the Bell Tolls / 170

Appendix

　　　　Kings and Queens Since 1066 / 174
　　　　Kings and Queens Since 1066 / 176

主要参考书目 / 178

Unit One

History

Section A Braveheart
Section B The Patriot
Section C Pearl Harbor

Preface

We live in an age of information and mass media. Serving as a blessing, film is one of the greatest tools that we have at our disposal, which is an especially powerful medium in providing visual representations of abstract and distant historical concepts.

This unit highlights three historical concepts predominantly: *Braveheart* introduces us a heroic figure during the Wars of Scottish Independence between England and Scotland in the 13th and 14th centuries; *The Patriot* focuses on the story happening on the eve of American Independence War in the 1770s; as the movie name indicates, *Pearl Harbor* is a film of epic and romance focusing on the attack on Pearl Harbor in World War II.

Unit Goals

- To have a basic knowledge about British history;
- To have a deep understanding of the causes of the American War of Independence;
- To be able to appraise the historical impact of the attack on Pearl Harbor.

Section A Braveheart

> Every man dies. Not every man really lives.
> —William Wallace

I. Warm-up Questions

1. How did England get its name?
2. When did the present United Kingdom come into being?
3. Do you know anything about William Wallace?

II. Basics about the Movie

Genre: epic, history, war
Director: Mel Gibson
Starring: Mel Gibson
　　　　　Sophie Marceau
　　　　　Patrick McGoohan
Release Year: 1995
Running Time: 178 minutes
Country: the United States

III. Synopsis

Mel Gibson's *Braveheart* is a full-throated, red-blooded battle epic about William Wallace, the legendary Scottish warrior who led his nation into battle against the English in the years around 1300s.

The movie begins from the year 1280 when the king of Britain, King Edward "Longshanks", invades and conquers Scotland following the death of Alexander III of

Scotland, who leaves no heir to the throne. Young William Wallace is a commoner and is taken abroad for education after the death of his father and brother.

Years later, the England king grants his noblemen land and privileges in Scotland, which arouses the local people's resistance, especially *Prima Nocte*. At the same time, the grown Wallace returns home and falls in love with his childhood friend Murron and they marry secretly. His newly-wedded wife is finally captured and publicly executed after her second attempt at defying the King's order. The furious Wallace leads his clan to slaughter the English garrison in his hometown.

Wallace rebels against England, and as his legend spreads, hundreds of Scots from the surrounding clans join him. Longshanks sends his son Prince Edward to stop Wallace by any every possible means. Wallace has a great victory at the Battle of Stirling Bridge and then destroys the city of York and kills the king's nephew. Robert the Bruce, the son of nobleman Robert the Elder and a contender for the Scottish crown, offers a false coalition with Wallace and his intention is detected by Wallace. Longshanks sends his son's wife Isabella of France on a negotiation mission and at the same time prepares for an abrupt attack.

Isabella is entranced by Wallace and warns him of the incoming invasion. Wallace appeals to the Scottish nobility to take up their arms and fight for their lost land. Longshanks confronts Wallace in the battle and wins the upper hand due to the betrayal of two Scottish traitors. Robert the Bruce stops Wallace from pursuing Langshanks and brings him to a safety place. Later, Wallace continues his guerrilla war against England for seven years, during which Wallace develops a romance with Isabella.

Wallace is set up and captured when he has a meeting with Robert. When Robert learns that his father, together with other nobles has handed over Wallace to the English, he breaks with his father. Isabella can also do nothing to save Wallace; however, she confides to the dying Longshanks that she is pregnant with Wallace's child.

Wallace is tried in public in London. He refuses to submit to the King or beg for mercy and is mercilessly beheaded. Later, Robert leads the army to continue their battle against England and they eventually win freedom for Scots.

Ⅳ. Culture Links

1. A Brief History of the United Kingdom

The earliest Britain inhabitants are said to be Mediterranean people who, during the prehistoric period, migrated through the English Channel and settled down. At about 2500 BC, Beaker folk came and they left Britain a mysterious scenic spot—Stonehenge. Subsequently, Britain was invaded by the Celts, the Romans, the Anglo-Saxons, the Vikings and the Normans and later was transformed from an absolute monarchy to a constitutional monarchy.

It is believed that between 1500 and 500 BC Celtic tribes migrated from Central Europe and France to Britain and settled down with the indigenous inhabitants. The Romans tried to invade Britain in 55 BC under Julius Caesar, but weren't successful until 43 AD, during the reign of Emperor Claudius Ⅰ(克劳狄一世). The Roman rule of Britain ended in 410 AD.

After the Romans left, three Germanic tribes—the Anglos, the Saxons, and the Jutes ruled Britain. They enslaved, killed or drove the Celts to the mountains. They established 7 kingdoms, ruling over all England from about 500 to 850 AD, which were later known as the Anglo-Saxon heptarchy(七国). The country got its name England, "the land of the Anglos".

At the end of the 8th century, the seven kingdoms got united under Alfred the Great (阿尔弗雷德大帝) in resisting the attacks from the Vikings. Wars continued and powers shifted during the next 130 years.

The Normans conquered Britain in 1066 when Duke William of Normandy challenged the successor of Edward the Confessor, Harold, and killed him at the battle of Hastings. The Norman Conquest is the last invasion of Britain from the alien nations.

After the Normans, Britain witnessed the rule of the House of Anjou(安茹王朝, 1154—1485), also known as the House of Plantagenet(金雀花王朝,1154—1399), during which period the *Magna Carta*(《大宪章》) was signed under the rule of King John in 1215. The *Magna Carta* granted the townspeople freedom of trade and self-government and compelled the king to rule by law. Therefore, it is regarded as the foundation of the British constitutionalism.

The Hundred Years' War(1337—1453) between England and France and the Wars of the Roses(1455—1485) between two noble families broke out during the 14th century and the 15th centuries. After the House of York(约克王朝) and the House of Lancaster(兰卡斯特王朝), England began its rule of the Tudors(都铎王朝,1485—1603).

Britain began the Reformation during the reign of the second monarch of the House of Tudor, Henry Ⅷ. He declared a break with the Roman Catholic Church and announced himself to be the Supreme Head of the Church of England (also called the Anglican Church).

The reign of the Stuarts(斯图亚特王朝,1603—1649,1660—1714) was interrupted as a result of the Civil Wars. Britain was a republic without a king or queen during the interval and the monarchy was restored with the Glorious Revolution. In 1689, *The Bill of Rights*(《权利法案》) was passed and the power of the monarch was limited.

Britain experienced the first Industrial Revolution from 1760 to 1840 during the House of Hanover(汉诺威王朝,1714—1901). As a result of it, Britain became the most advanced industrial country in the world. Under the reign of Queen Victoria, Britain's prosperity reached its climax and its colonies were worldwide.

The Windsors(温莎王朝,1917—)① began to reign at the beginning of the 20th century and witnessed the decline in influence after World War Ⅰ and World War Ⅱ. In the 20th century, the United States took the place of the United Kingdom as the strongest and richest country in the world.②

▶ 2. England and Scotland

The full name of Britain is the United Kingdom of Great Britain and Northern Ireland, or the UK for short. England and Scotland are two components of the UK, and the other two are Wales and Northern Ireland, but in history Scotland was once an independent country.

A tribe of the Celts called Scots came to the northern part of Britain and established a country called Scotland. In 843 AD, the Kingdom of Scotland came into being and it remained an independent sovereign state for hundreds of years. Wars broke out frequently between the Kingdom of England and the Kingdom of Scotland in the 13th and 14th centuries. During the Wars of Scottish Independence (1296—1328), William Wallace emerged as the principal leader of the resistance to English rule and became a Scottish hero. In 1603, the two countries shared the same ruler but still remained interdependent. It was not until 1707 that the Kingdom of Scotland agreed to enter into a political union with the

---

① 温莎王朝前身为萨克森—科堡-哥达王朝,因"一战"而引起人们对德国的抵制,1917年改为现名。

② All the dynasties and the monarchs in Britain since 1066 are listed in the end of the book. Please refer to Appendix for further references.

Kingdom of England to create a new Kingdom of Great Britain.

On Sept. 18, 2014, the Scotland held a national referendum to decide whether to break the 307-year union and go it alone as an independent nation or to stick with the United Kingdom. The poll revealed that 55% of Scottish people chose to stay with the UK; the referendum ended with Scotland still being a member of the UK.

V. Exercises

Multiple Choices: *Choose the best answer from the four choices given.*

1. *Braveheart* is an epic war film directed and starred by a world-famous _____, Mel Gibson.

   A. Briton   B. Scot   C. Australian   D. American

2. What is the direct reason for William Wallace's rebel against England?

   A. The death of his father and brother.   B. The education he received.

   C. The cruelty of the English king.   D. The death of his wife.

3. Which of the following sentences is not taken from *Braveheart*?

   A. Use your brain before the sword.

   B. Fear can hold you prisoner; hope can set you free.

   C. Every man dies. Not every man really lives.

   D. Your heart is free. Have the courage to follow it.

4. Which of the following words cannot be used to describe Robert the Bruce?

   A. Ambitious.   B. Treacherous.   C. Well-to-do.   D. Helpful.

5. Which of the following never invaded England?

   A. The Vikings.   B. The Germany.

   C. The Romans.   D. The Anglo-Saxons.

6. Which of the following statements about Scotland is NOT true?

   A. Of all the four districts in the UK, Scotland is the second largest in terms of land, only second to England.

   B. Scotland is famous for its kilts, bagpipes and whisky.

   C. Scotland has been a sovereign country since 1714.

   D. Scotland lost its chance of being an independent country in 2014 referendum.

Unit One History

7. The House of Anjou was also called _____ in history.
   A. the House of York   B. the House of Lancaster
   C. the House of Hanover   D. the House of Plantagenet
8. _____ is regarded as the foundation of the British constitutionalism.
   A. *The Magna Carta*   B. The Norman Conquest
   C. *The Bill of Rights*   D. The Reformation

▶ **Blank-filling**: *Fill in the blanks with the missing information.*
1. *Braveheart* is an epic directed by _____, who also stars the protagonist, a _____ warrior and hero.
2. In the movie Braveheart refers to _____, who rises up and leads his country men to fight against _____ and finally sacrifices his own life.
3. England was invaded by many foreign invaders in history, such as _____, _____, and _____.
4. The rights of the king was first limited by _____ under the reign of _____, and it was further restrained by _____ after the Glorious Revolution.
5. Scotland used to be an independent country during the year _____ to _____. In recent years, the Scottish government and the United Kingdom government reached an agreement and more than 4,300,000 voters participated in the referendum in _____.

▶ **Translate & Appreciate**: *Translate the classic lines from the movie into Chinese and share your understandings.*
1. Your heart is free. Have the courage to follow it.

   _____
   _____

2. Men don't follow titles. They follow courage.

   _____
   _____

3. Freedom is the best, I tell thee true, of all things to be won. Then never live within the bond of slavery, my son.

   _____
   _____
   _____
   _____

4. Fight, and you may die. Run, and you'll live at least a while. And dying in your beds many years from now. Would you be willing to trade? All the days from this day to that, for one chance, just one chance, to come back here and tell our enemies that they may take our lives, but they'll never take our Freedom! Freedom—

_____
_____
_____
_____

▶ **Voice Your Opinion**: *Read the following reviews about Braveheart and voice your opinions on this movie after you finish watching it.*

⟨1⟩

Braveheart received much criticism from certain History Buffs upon its release. They said that the filmmakers portrayed Scotsman William Wallace as a brave, heroic, good man. History Buffs, however, said that he was just as vicious as the English and spared no one. Well, thank you for that, Mr. History Teacher(s). If I wanted to learn about history I wouldn't be going to see a movie starring Mel Gibson, with the tagline "Every man dies. Not every man really lives," would I? I enjoyed every inch of *Braveheart*, and if I wanted a history lesson, I'd go to see *Gods and Generals*, which turned out to be a horrible film— which just goes to show that historical accuracy can sometimes break a film and not make it.

Gibson plays William Wallace, a Scot who decides to revolt against the England after his wife was killed by a pack of the thieving scoundrels! The film is LOOSELY based on his life—since no one really knows much about Wallace other than what he did: free Scotland from the English for a while (when I say "for a while", it is because their "free-e-e-edom!" only lasted for a while…), so much of the story is made up. But as I said, I'm not looking for a history lesson when I go to see a movie like this.

This is a first director outing for Gibson, who not only gives us one of his best—if not the best—performance of his career, other than those great *Lethal Weapon* movies! He handles the direction very well for an actor-turned-director. He doesn't try anything memorable—no fancy camera sweeps to make us motion sick—but he directs the film like the old epics, one of many great things about the film.

The cinematography is excellent. I can't think of another film that is quite so beautiful to behold. It is truly wonderful to watch the surroundings fly by the screen, purely unadulterated.

Unit One　History

　　As for Gibson's Scottish accent... well... he speaks surprisingly well with a Scottish accent, and doesn't sound like an American-Australian phony (Isn't he an Aussie?). There is a great supporting cast in this film, as well, with a man in a rubber nose that you might not be able to place at first glance...

　　James Horner's magnificent score is truly marvelous to behold. He mixes Scottish bagpipes and emotion into a little bundle, which makes you feel emotional. It plays during the film at just the right moments and makes it easier to feel elated or depressed.

　　All in all, I think that *Braveheart* stands as one of the best films I have ever seen. It is an epic in all sense of the word; I don't care how historically incorrect it is. If I wanted a history lesson, I wouldn't be going to see a film like this.

Key points: _____

_____

_____

_____

_____

〈2〉

　　Braveheart is quite simply, one of the best and most successful movies ever created and a huge part of that success comes from the efforts extended by Mel Gibson, as he wore three different hats for this masterpiece, those being producer, director and star. The one oddity about this movie for me was that I pretty much wore out my VHS copy of it and had, a couple years ago, purchased the DVD but only just recently took the opportunity to watch it again and no matter how many times you watch this movie, it is still a stunning, compelling and extraordinarily intriguing film that draws you into the life of William Wallace despite already knowing how it's going to end.

　　The one thing that drives this movie is the spirit that Mel Gibson puts into his character of William Wallace and it is no surprise that *Braveheart* won five Academy Awards, including Best Picture of 1995 and Best Director for Mel Gibson. The only true surprise is that he wasn't among the top five nominated for or won the Best Actor award.

　　High praise also goes to the long list of supporting actors and actresses that starred in this superb film! The most notable was the performance by Sophie Marceau, one of the most beautiful women on the planet. Patrick McGoohan was absolutely incredible in the role of the villain Longshanks, King Edward I, delivering a memorable performance.

　　One of the most notable performances in this film, among the many, was the work done by James Horner who was responsible for the score. As is normally the case when his name appears in the credits, everything about the score, from the first reel to the last, is incredibly well blended into the movie and serves extremely well in enhancing the experience of the movie.

The Premise:

As the old saying goes, is it Hollywood or History? The truth is, of course it's a bit of history, put together Hollywood style to make one of the best films ever presented to the audience. The truth behind it is that we'll never know as recorded history from this era is circumspect as best. Where a huge portion of the credit for this film lays is in the hands of Randall Wallace, a descendant of William Wallace's.

As this historic film opens, we see a young William Wallace in Scotland as he's learning the harsh lessons of life in his era. After his family is killed in battle he's fortunate enough to have his Uncle Argyle (played brilliantly by Brian Cox) take him under his wing! Several years later he returns home to find that his countrymen are still suffering under the yoke of English oppression but he didn't come home for that. He came home for Murron MacClannough (Catherine McCormack), seeking her hand in marriage. Unfortunate events unfold from there and William loses the love of his life and goes on a rampage not only to avenge his love but to free his country…

What follows from there is not only one of the best films of the nineties but one of the best films of all times. I highly recommend *Braveheart* to any and all who are interested in seeing what true movie making is about!

Key points: _____

_____
_____
_____
_____

Think about the following questions "How do you like the movie *Braveheart*?" "What is the acceptable treatment of history in movies?" before putting down your own reviews of the movie.

Your opinion: _____

_____
_____
_____
_____
_____

Unit One   History

Section B   The Patriot

> The honor is found in the end, not the means.
> —The Patriot

I. Warm-up Questions

1. What was the cause of the American War of Independence?
2. Who drafted *The Declaration of Independence*? When is American Independence Day?
3. How much do you know about Mel Gibson? What is his latest movie?

II. Basics about the Movie

Genre: epic, history, war
Director: Roland Emmerich
Starring: Mel Gibson
　　　　　Heath Ledger
　　　　　Joely Richardson
Running Time: 164 minutes
Release Year: 2000
Country: the United States

III. Synopsis

During the American Revolution in 1776, Benjamin Martin, a veteran of the French and Indian War and a widower with seven children, is called to Charleston to vote in the South Carolina General Assembly on a levy supporting the Continental Army. Fearing war against Great Britain, Benjamin refuses to vote. The vote is passed and, against his father's wishes, Benjamin's eldest son Gabriel joins the Continental Army.

Two years later, the ruthless Colonel William Tavington arrives, arrests Gabriel, and takes captive the African American free men and women who work on Benjamin's land. Tavington kills Thomas, Benjamin's second son, and then orders the Martin's house burned, and the wounded Americans killed. After the British leave, Benjamin gives his next two eldest sons rifles, and they attack the British unit escorting a tied Gabriel. Benjamin skillfully, yet brutally, kills many soldiers with his tomahawk. Benjamin and Gabriel make a definite decision to fight the British.

Gabriel asks why Villeneuve and others mention Benjamin's role in something called "Fort Wilderness". Benjamin says that when he was fighting in the British army in the French and Indian War he and several other soldiers were sent on a mission to attack a French fort called "Fort Wilderness" where he and his comrades literally cut the defending French soldiers apart slowly, revealing why Benjamin is always hesitant when asked about the event and why he is haunted by his past.

Tavington learns the identities of some militia members and proceeds to attack their families and burn their homes. Benjamin's family flees to live in a Gullah settlement with former black slaves. There, Gabriel marries his betrothed Anne. Tavington rides into the town and assembles all the townspeople, including Anne, into the church promising freedom in exchange for the whereabouts of the rebels. However, after revealing the location, the people are trapped as Tavington orders the church burned. After discovering the tragedy, Gabriel and several others race to attack Tavington's encampment. In the ensuing fight, Tavington mortally wounds Gabriel before fleeing. Benjamin arrives soon after, only to have another of his sons die in his arms.

Benjamin mourns and makes his commitment to continue fighting. The British appear to have the upper hand until Benjamin rallies the troops forward against their lines and Tavington rushes to personally target him. Tavington gains the upper hand, delivering several wounds to Benjamin. At the last second, however, Benjamin avoids the attack and kills Tavington, avenging his sons' deaths.

Ⅳ. Culture Links

 1. The American People

The population experienced a quick growth in Britain's 13 North American colonies in the 18th century. In 1700 the population was about 250,000; seven decades later there were about 2,500,000 inhabitants. This growth of population was a prior condition for a successful independence movement.

The American population also changed in composition. The proportion of the inhabitants with English culture and ancestry declined during the 1700s because of the migration of new racial and ethnic groups. Many people came from Germany, Scotland, and Ireland and settled in their own communities. In 1775 about one-fifth of the people of the mainland colonies were of African ancestry. Unlike Latin America and the West Indies, North American slaves had a high rate of natural increase. About 250,000 Africans were brought to the mainland colonies before 1775, but the total black population numbered 567,000 on the eve of independence.

This growth in population and diversity made it more difficult for Britain to rule the American colonies.

2. The Development of Economy in North America

In addition to the rapid growth and diversity of the population, the prosperous agricultural and commercial economy in the colonies during the 18th century helped the success of the independence movement. This economic system incorporated the production of wheat, cattle, corn, tobacco, and rice exported to the West Indies, Britain, and Europe.

The two most important trade routes, namely, the tobacco and the sugar trades were controlled by British merchants; American merchants dominated two small trade routes: the export of rice to Europe and the export of supplies from the Northern mainland to the West Indies. However, American control of these trade routes hurt the British business, which depended on raw materials from the colonies that were shipped to Great Britain and then exported as finished products. The British discouraged any colonial trade except with Great Britain.

The colonists' participation in transatlantic trade triggered the rise of the American port cities of Boston, New York, Philadelphia, Baltimore, Newport, and Charleston which later became the birthplaces of the independence movement.

3. British Power in the Colonies

At the end of the Seven Years' War (1756—1763), Great Britain stood triumphant among western European powers. But the war had been expensive, and the colonies had seemed insubordinate and uncooperative, even though colonials gloried in being Britons.

After 1763 successive British administrations tried to tax the colonies directly to pay for the defense and administration and to maintain Parliament's power. The Revenue or *Sugar*

Act(《食糖法》,1764) taxed all sugar and molasses brought to the mainland colonies. Despite the protests and a great deal of smuggling, it was implemented. The *Stamp Act* (《印花税法案》,1765) tried to tap colonial business by requiring official stamps on most transactions. *The Stamp Act* triggered colonial resistance which invalidated the Act everywhere except Georgia, and it was abolished in 1766. The *Declaratory Act*(《宣示法案》,1766) announced that Parliament could legislate for the colonies "in all cases whatsoever". In 1767 the *Townshend Acts*(《汤森法案》) taxed imported glass, lead, paint, paper and tea. Resistance triggered the abolishment of all except the tea duty in 1770.

After 1767 an American Board of Customs Commissioners was based in Boston. Troops were stationed there in 1768 to protect customs officials. In 1773 Parliament implemented the tea tax to rescue the bankrupt East India Company by letting it market tea directly to America. Most towns simply turned the tea ships around before they entered the port limits and had to declare their cargoes. But Boston could not. When intense negotiations about sending it back finally failed on 16 December 1773, "Mohawks[①]" dumped the tea into the Harbor. This was the Boston Tea Party(波士顿倾茶事件), which has been seen as helping to spark the American Revolution.

4. The First Continental Congress

The First Continental Congress was a meeting of delegates from twelve of the Thirteen Colonies that met on September 5 to October 26, 1774, at Carpenters' Hall in Philadelphia, Pennsylvania, early in the American Revolution. It was called in response to "the passage of the *Coercive Acts*(《强制法令》)" (also known as "*Intolerable Acts*(《不可容忍法令》)" by the colonial Americans) by the British Parliament. The *Intolerable Acts* had punished Massachusetts for the Boston Tea Party.

The Congress was attended by 56 delegates. The Pennsylvania delegation was appointed by the colonial assembly. Georgia declined to send delegates because they were hoping for British assistance with native American problems on their frontier and did not want to offend the British.

The Congress met briefly to consider options, including an economic boycott of British

---

① 莫霍克人,北美印第安人的一个种族。

trade and drawing up a list of rights and grievances; in the end, they petitioned King George Ⅲ for redress of those grievances.

Their petition was proved to be unsuccessful in halting enforcement of the *Intolerable Acts*. Their appeal to the Crown had no effect, and so the Second Continental Congress was held the following year to organize the defense of the colonies at the onset of the American Revolutionary War. The delegates also urged each colony to set up and train its own militia.

5. The War of Independence/American Revolutionary War (1775—1783)

On April 19, 1775, some British soldiers were sent to Concord to search for weapons and "rebels". When the troops reached Lexington at dawn, they encountered militiamen. Fighting broke out and the first shots in the American War of Independence were fired.

In May 1775, the Second Continental Congress was held in Philadelphia and acted as a provisional government of the 13 colony-states. It established the Continental Army and Navy under the command of George Washington. Thomas Jefferson (1743—1826) drafted *The Declaration of Independence*, which the Congress adopted on July 4, 1776. The Declaration presented a public defense of the American War of Independence, and most importantly, it explained the philosophy behind the war, that men have a natural right to "Life, Liberty and the pursuit of Happiness", that governments can rule only with "the consent of the governed", that any government may be dissolved when it fails to protect the rights of the people. This theory of politics is central to the Western political tradition.

At first, the war went badly for the Americans. After endless hard fighting, in October 1777, the Americans won a great victory at Saratoga. This was the turning point of the war, leading to an alliance between the US and France. Finally, in 1781, the Americans won a decisive victory at Yorktown. On October 19, 1781, the British soldiers were forced to surrender. In 1783 the British and the Americans signed the *Treaty of Paris*(《美英巴黎条约》), and the United States of America won its independence.

6. *The Declaration of Independence*

The Declaration of Independence, perhaps the most famous document in American history, was used by the 13 British North American colonies to declare their independence from Great Britain. *The Declaration of Independence* was adopted in final form on July 4,

1776. The preparation of the declaration began on June 11, when the Congress appointed a committee composed of Thomas Jefferson, John Adams, Benjamin Franklin, Robert R. Livingston, and Roger Sherman. Jefferson actually wrote the declaration.

Jefferson's famous phrase concerning "Life, Liberty, and the pursuit of Happiness" is a slight reworking of the wording of Virginia declaration. His draft was made several changes by the Congress, yet the document remained an expression of the liberal political ideas.

It can be divided into three parts: a statement of principle concerning the rights of man and the legitimacy of revolution, a list of specific grievances against England's King George Ⅲ, and a formal claim of independence.

The document transformed the colonists' struggle with Great Britain from a defense of their rights as Englishmen to a revolution aimed at overthrowing the existing form of government. Different from the *Articles of Confederation*(《邦联条例》) or the *Constitution of the United States*, it did not establish a structure of government. For the American colonists, the declaration was an announcement to the rest of the world that the colonies were independent from Great Britain; it also provided a rationale for this action. The goal was to get internal support united for their struggle and to encourage external assistance from European powers such as France.

Ⅴ. Exercises

▶ **True or False Statements**: *Read the following statements and decide whether they are true (T) or false (F).*

　　_____ 1. *The Patriot* depicts the story of an American who swept into the Civil War when his family was threatened.

　　_____ 2. *The Patriot* is a 2000 American epic historical fiction war film directed by Roland Emmerich, and starring Mel Gibson.

　　_____ 3. The War of Independence lasted for 8 years, during which *The Declaration of Independence* was issued.

　　_____ 4. George Washington drafted *The Declaration of Independence*, which the Congress adopted on July 4, 1776.

　　_____ 5. The First Continental Congress was a meeting of delegates from thirteen colonies that met on September 5 to October 26, 1774.

　　_____ 6. The growth in population and diversity in culture made an important

Unit One　History

precondition for the rise of an independence movement.

_____ 7. The emergence of a prosperous agricultural and commercial economy in the colonies during the 18th century helped pave the way for the independence movement.

_____ 8. The turning point of the War of Independence came at Gettysburg.

_____ 9. The Boston Tea Party helped spark the American War of Independence.

_____ 10. The Second Continental Congress drew up a list of rights and grievances; in the end, they petitioned King George Ⅲ for redress of those grievances.

▶ **Short-answer Questions**: *Give brief answers to the following questions.*

1. When did the War of Independence begin and end?

2. What are the causes of the American War of Independence?

3. What is the historical impact of *The Declaration of Independence*?

4. What is the philosophy behind the American War of Independence?

▶ **Extracurricular Exploration**: *Watch the movie and explore the Internet. Find out the answers to the following questions and make a no-more-than-5-minute presentation.*

1. Which character in the movie impresses you most? Why? Could you pick out any part to illustrate this person's character?

2. Are there any other historical events included in the film besides the American War of Independence?

3. Surf the Internet. Find more information about the American War of Independence and share it with the class.

Section C Pearl Harbor

Ⅰ. Movie Information (Explore and Find)

Genre: _____
Chinese Title: _____
Director: _____
Starring: _____
Running Time: 183 minutes
Release Year: _____
Country: _____
Awards: _____

▶ Use the information you have found to fill in the blanks.

Pearl Harbor is a _____ (year) _____ (country) _____ (genre) film directed by _____, produced by Bay and Jerry Bruckheimer and written by Randall Wallace. It stars _____, _____, _____, etc. The film is loosely based on the _____ in December 1941, and the Doolittle Raid.

Despite receiving generally negative reviews from critics, the film was a major box office success, earning $59 million in its opening weekend and, in the end, nearly $450 million worldwide. It was nominated for _____ Academy Awards, winning in the category of _____. However, it was also nominated for six Golden Raspberry Awards, including _____, _____, _____, etc. This marked the first occurrence of a Worst-Picture-nominated film winning an Academy Award.

Ⅱ. Synopsis

Growing up together, Danny and Rafe are inseparable best friends. In January 1941, Danny and Rafe are both first lieutenants under the command of Major Jimmy Doolittle. Doolittle informs Rafe that he has been accepted into the Eagle Squadron (an RAF outfit for

Unit One History

American pilots during the Battle of Britain). Rafe flies in numerous dogfights with the RAF against the German Air Force, but he is shot down over the English Channel and presumed to be killed in action. Danny gives Evelyn, the girlfriend of Rafe, the news and she is heartbroken. Three months later, Evelyn and Danny begin to develop feelings for each other and the two begin a relationship.

On the night of December 6, Evelyn is shocked to discover Rafe survived his shoot-down over the Channel. Danny finds Rafe in the bar with the intention of making things right, but the two get into a fight.

Early the next morning, on December 7, 1941, the Japanese navy begins its attack on Pearl Harbor. Danny and Rafe drive away in search of a still standing airfield, while Evelyn and the other nurses rush for the hospital. The nurses struggle to give emergency treatment to hundreds of injured. Rafe and Danny manage to get in the air and fight against Japanese air force. After causing four planes to crash into each other and another getting shot down by ground fire, the two shoot down seven Japanese Zeros.

The next day, President Franklin Delano Roosevelt delivers his Day of Infamy Speech to the nation and requests the US Congress to declare a state of war with Japan. Later, both Danny and Rafe arrive in California for a secret mission which involves bombing Tokyo and then landing in China. However, Danny is shot by Japanese when they carry out the mission. Rafe tells Danny that Evelyn is pregnant and he must live to be his father. Danny then tells Rafe that he will have to be the father and dies. Back in California, a pregnant Evelyn sees Rafe getting off the aircraft, carrying Danny's coffin. After the war, Rafe and Evelyn, now married, visit Danny's grave with Danny and Evelyn's son, also named Danny. Rafe then asks his son if he would like to go flying, and they fly off into the sunset in the old biplane that his father once had.

 III. Culture Links

The film is loosely based on the Japanese attack on Pearl Harbor, and the Doolittle Raid. Please supply the missing information.

▶ 1. America in the Days of World War II

In the early days of World War II, the US government adopted a _____ policy. The American capitalists wanted to continue their profitable trade with the warring countries, including the aggressors.

The American policy underwent great changes in 1940. In Europe, the British had

19

been driven out to the continent and suffered repeated air raids by _____. In Asia, _____ had openly announced its "New Order" in an attempt to extend its control to the Pacific. The American government began to fear that _____ were winning the war and that their victory would threaten America's security and interests.

_____ was the direct cause for America's entrance into the war. On _____, Japanese planes suddenly showered bombs on the American fleet and military installations at _____, Hawaii. About 3,400 Americans were killed or wounded, with the loss of more than 180 planes and eight battleships. A few minutes later, Japan declared war on America and the US government responded by declaring war against Japan the following day.

In June 1944, _____, _____ and Canadian forces landed on the beaches of Normandy, opening the long-delayed western front to attack _____. In _____, Germany surrendered. On August 6 and 9, American airplanes dropped two _____ bombs on Hiroshima and Nagasaki. On August 14, _____ surrendered and the World War Ⅱ ended.

In April 1945, a conference was called in _____ (city) to organize the United Nations. _____ countries altogether attended the conference and the United Nations was established.

2. The Doolittle Raid

The Doolittle Raid, also known as the Tokyo Raid, on _____, was an air raid by _____ on the Japanese capital _____ and other places on the island of Honshu during World War Ⅱ, the first air strike to strike the Japanese Home Islands. It demonstrated that Japan itself was vulnerable to American air attack, served as _____ for the Japanese attack on Pearl Harbor, and provided an important boost to American morale. The raid was planned and led by _____.

The raid caused negligible material damage to Japan, but it achieved its goal of raising American morale and casting doubt in Japan on the ability of its military leaders to defend their Home Islands.

3. Franklin Delano Roosevelt

Franklin Delano Roosevelt (January 30, 1882—April 12, 1945), commonly known as FDR, was an American _____ who served as the _____ President of the United

Unit One　History

States from _____ until his death in _____. A Democrat, he won a record of four presidential elections and emerged as a central figure in world events during the mid-20th century. He directed the United States government during most of the Great Depression and _____. He is often rated by scholars as one of the three greatest US presidents, along with _____ and _____.

IV. Expansion

Explore the Internet. Find out the answers to the following questions and make a no-more-than-5-minute presentation.

1. *Tora! Tora! Tora!* is a 1970 Japanese-American biographical war film that dramatizes the Japanese attack on Pearl Harbor. What are the differences between *Pearl Harbor* and *Tora! Tora! Tora!*?

2. War and love are two eternal topics in the literature and film. How does this movie portray the two topics? Do you think the film has fulfilled the job in a successful way? Give your own reasons.

V. Fun Time

Now listen to the song *There You'll Be*, a super movie hit by Faith Hill. It was released in May 2001 and was featured on the *Pearl Harbor* soundtrack.

There You'll Be
By Faith Hill

When I think back on these times,

And the dreams we left behind

I'll be glad 'cause I was blessed to get to have you in my life

When I look back on those days
I'll look and see your face
You were right there for me

In my dreams, I'll always see you soar above the sky
In my heart, there'll always be a place for you
For all my life, I'll keep a part of you with me
And everywhere I am there you'll be

Well, you showed me how it feels the sky I reach
And I will always remember all the strength you gave to me
Your love made me make it through
Oh, I owe so much to you
You were right there for me

In my dreams, I'll always see you soar above the sky
In my heart, there'll always be a place for you
For all my life, I'll keep a part of you with me
And everywhere I am there you'll be

'cause I always saw in you my life, my strength
And I wanna thank you now for all the ways
You were right there for me
You were right there for me

In my dreams, I'll always see you soar above the sky
In my heart, there'll always be a place for you
For all my life, I'll keep a part of you with me
And everywhere I am there you'll be
And everywhere I am there you'll be
There you'll be

Unit Two

Religion

Section A   Brideshead Revisited
Section B   Se7en
Section C   Noah

Preface

Religion had been the most important component of Western culture, and also a rooted faith and reliance to the Western people before Friedrich Nietzsche declared "God is dead" in the last century.

In this unit, let's get closer to three movies and gain an insight into the mysterious religion in British and America. Section A introduces *Brideshead Revisited*, which explores themes including nostalgia for the age of English aristocracy and the influence of Catholicism; Section B illustrates *Se7en* whose main theme is sin and in particular, the seven deadly sins of gluttony, greed, sloth, lust, pride, envy and anger; Section C is about a film inspired by the story of Noah's Ark from the Book of Genesis.

Unit Goals

➤ To have a deep understanding of the Reformation and the coming of the Church of England;

➤ To understand the characteristics of religion in the United States;

➤ To have a general idea of the story of Noah building an ark.

Section A Brideshead Revisited

> I should like to bury something precious in every place where I've been happy and then, when I was old and ugly and miserable, I could come back and dig it up and remember.
>
> —Sebastian

Ⅰ. Warm-up Questions

1. What is the main religion in Britain?

2. Do you know the meaning of the following terms such as the Roman Catholic, the Anglican, Christianity, Protestants, and Puritans?

3. How much do you know about the Reformation?

Ⅱ. Basics about the Movie

Genre: drama
Director: Julian Jarrold
Starring: Emma Thompson
  Matthew Goode
  Ben Whishaw
Running Time: 133 minutes
Release Year: 2008
Country: the United Kingdom, Italy, Morocco

Unit Two　Religion

 III. **Synopsis**

Brideshead Revisited is a movie based on the novel by the English writer Evelyn Waugh under the title of *Brideshead Revisited*, *The Sacred & Profane Memories of Captain Charles Ryder*. The movie is mainly about the romance between the narrator Charles Ryder and the brother and sister from a Catholic family during the 1920s to 1940s.

Charles Ryder studies history at Hertford College of Oxford and he is befriended by Sebastian Flyte from Christ Church. He gets the invitation to Sebastian's home, a grand abbey known as Brideshead, where he also knows Sebastian's family, including his mother Lady Marchmain, a devout Roman Catholic, and his younger sister Julia.

Sebastian's father, Lord Marchmain, had converted from Anglicanism to Roman Catholicism to marry his wife, but he later abandoned both his marriage and his new religion, and moved to Venice, Italy. Charles is encouraged to visit Lord Marchmain with the brother and sister by Lady Marchmain who hopes that he can act as a positive influence on Sebastian. During this visit, Charles ends his friendship with Sebastian and Lady Marchmain also makes it clear that Charles cannot marry Julia since he is an atheist.

Sebastian is so addicted to alcoholism that his mother cancels his allowance. One day when he arrives drunk with the money from Charles and worst of all, improperly dressed at a ball celebrating Julia's engagement, Lady Marchmain puts all the blames on Charles. As a consequence, Sebastian flees to Morocco and is hopelessly taken ill.

Years later, Charles becomes a married successful painter and he meets Julia unexpectedly on an ocean liner traveling to England from New York. They realize they are still on the mind of each other, so Charles returns to Brideshead to persuade Julia's husband Rex to step aside, whose response shocks and angers Julia. Without warning, the dying Lord Marchmain arrives at Brideshead to spend his final days. On his deathbed Lord Marchmain regains his faith and dies reconciled to the Roman Catholic Church. Deeply affected by her father's transformation, Julia decides she cannot abandon her own faith to marry Charles, and they part.

Several years later during the Second World War, once again Charles steps in Brideshead. Things are different: this time Charles is not a visitor but an army captain; Brideshead is no longer a luxurious abbey but a military base…

Ⅳ. Culture Links

1. Religion in the UK

The United Kingdom is composed of four parts: England, Scotland, Wales and Northern Ireland; each part retains its capital, national anthem and national flag. The same is true to their religious beliefs.

The official religion of England is **Christianity**(基督教), as practiced by **the Anglican Church of England**(英格兰圣公会,英国国教). The Church in Wales is also Anglican. In Scotland the official Church is the Presbyterian Church(长老会教派) of Scotland. Other Christians in each country also include the Roman Catholics(天主教) and the Methodists(循道会).

Britain is a multi faith society in which everyone is entitled to religious freedom. Although Britain is historically a Christian society, people are usually very tolerant towards the faiths of others and those who have no religious beliefs. The main religion in Britain is Christianity. Most Christians belong to the Church of England or the Church of Scotland. These are Protestant Churches(新教教会). There are also many Roman Catholics. The Queen (the British Monarch) is "Supreme Governor of the Church of England".

Although religious faith in Britain is predominantly Christian, most of the world's religions are also practiced. There are Islam(伊斯兰教), Hinduism(印度教), Judaism(犹太教), Buddhism(佛教), as well as Sikhism(锡克教), etc.

Many of England's most notable buildings and monuments are religious in nature, including the Stonehenge, the Angel of the North, Westminster Abbey, St. Paul's Cathedral and Canterbury Cathedral. The festivals of Christmas and Easter, both of which are religious in origin, are still widely commemorated in the country.

2. History of Religion in the UK

Pre-Roman forms of religion in Britain included various forms of ancestor worship and paganism. Little is known about the details of such religions. Forms of Christianity have dominated religious life in what is now the United Kingdom for over 1,400 years. It was introduced by the Romans to what are now England, Wales, and Southern Scotland.

During the Middle Ages, the Catholic Church remained the dominant form of Western Christianity in Britain, but the (Anglican) Church of England became the independently established church in England and Wales in 1534 as a result of the English Reformation.

In 1553, Mary became Queen. She changed the country back to Catholicism and burned Protestants who wouldn't change at the stake. In 1558, Elizabeth became Queen. She changed the church back to Anglican and it has been the official religion of England since.

In 1290, the Jews in England were expelled and only emancipated in the 19th century. British Jews numbered fewer than 10,000 in 1800 but around 120,000 after 1881 when Russian Jews settled permanently in Britain.

Since the 1920s, the substantial immigration to the United Kingdom has contributed to the growth of foreign faiths, especially of Islam, Hinduism and Sikhism. Buddhism in the United Kingdom experienced growth partly due to immigration and partly due to conversion.

3. Catholic Church

The Catholic Church is a denomination in Christianity. It is the largest denomination of Christians, with over 1 billion people in the Church. It teaches that it is the same Church started by Jesus Christ and his followers about 2,000 years ago. The headquarters of the Catholic Church is based in the Vatican (梵蒂冈).

Almost half of all Catholics are in Latin America. The second largest concentration is in Europe. Millions of Catholics live in other places all over the world.

The Catholic Church is led by the Pope, the Bishop of Rome, who lives in Vatican. According to Catholics, the Church is guided by the Holy Spirit, who also guides the Pope. The Church teaches that when the Pope speaks officially on the subject of Catholic faith and morals he cannot be wrong. The Catholic Church teaches that the first Pope was

Saint Peter. The current pope is Pope Francis.

Like other Christians, Catholics believe Jesus Christ is a divine person, the Son of God. They believe that because of his love for all people, he died so that all of us will live forever in heaven. The Catholic Church also recognizes the Trinity(三位一体), i. e. the Father, the Son and the Holy Spirit(圣父、圣子、圣灵) together are the only God. Catholics should follow the example of love Jesus Christ both teaches and gives: to love each other so much that one is even willing to die for another. Catholicism emphasizes that the Catholic Church is one true church. The Catholic Church claims that it is the only institution with knowledge of religious and moral law. Catholics even tend to promote intermarriage and the maintenance of their religious attachment and willingness to support their church with money.

Some of the traditional worship practices of Roman Catholics include making the sign of the cross, kneeling, bowing, and receiving the Eucharist(圣餐) during their worship ceremonies. Their main form of worship is called the Mass(弥撒). It is celebrated every day. Catholics are required to attend on Sunday and on a few Holy Days of obligation.

The Catholic Church celebrates seven sacraments(圣事): Baptism, Confirmation, Eucharist, Reconciliation, Anointing of the Sick, Holy Orders and Holy Matrimony (marriage)(洗礼圣事、坚振圣事、圣体圣事、忏悔圣事、病人傅油圣事、圣秩圣事、婚姻圣事). The Holy Eucharist is the most important of the sacraments, because Catholics believe that Jesus Christ becomes truly present in the form of bread and wine.

4. The Reformation and the Church of England (Anglican Church)

In the 16th century, there was a big change in the way some Christians worshipped God. In 1517, a German monk called Martin Luther led a breakaway from the Roman Catholic Church. The new Christians called themselves "Protestants"(新教徒) because they were protesting against the Roman "Catholic" Church, its teachings and its customs. Their demand for reform led to this period of history being called the **Reformation**(宗教改革).

England was a Catholic nation under the rule of Henry Ⅶ (1485—1509) and during much of Henry Ⅷ's (1509—1547) reign. When Henry Ⅷ came to the throne, he was a devout Catholic and defended the Church against Protestants.

However, when the Pope refused to grant Henry Ⅷ a divorce from Catherine of Aragon who failed to produce a male heir, Henry split off the English Church from the Roman Church. At that time, a divorce was not a simple issue. In fact, it was very complicated. Henry

Unit Two Religion

VIII was a Roman Catholic and the Roman Catholic faith believed in marriage for life. It did not recognize, let alone support, divorce. By 1533 Henry VIII's anger was such that he ordered the Archbishop of Canterbury to grant him a divorce so that he could marry Anne Boleyn. This event led to England breaking away from the Rome Catholic Church based in Rome. Henry placed himself as head of the church and in his eyes, his divorce was perfectly legal.

King Henry VIII issued *The Act of Supremacy*(《最高治权法案》) in 1534 and declared himself supreme head of the Church of England. This marked the start of centuries of religious conflict in Britain.

The year 1535 saw Henry ordering the closing down of Roman Catholic Abbeys, monasteries and convents across England, Wales and Ireland. This act became known as the "Dissolution of the Monasteries".

Until Henry's death in 1547, although England split off from Rome, it remained a Catholic country. It wasn't until Henry's son, Edward VI, and his advisors, that England became a Protestant country.

Henry's son Edward was given Protestant teachers and brought up as a strict protestant. Under King Edward VI (1547—1553), England became a Protestant nation. King Edward VI was a devout Protestant and introduced a new prayer book. All church services were held in English. Catholics were treated very badly and catholic bishops were locked up.

Under Queen Mary I (1553—1558), England was again a Catholic nation. Mary was a devout Catholic. The pope became the head of the church again. Church services were changed back to Latin. During the last three years of her reign, 300 leading Protestants who would not accept Catholic beliefs were burned to death at the stake.

Under Queen Elizabeth I (1558—1603), England was again a Protestant nation. It was under Elizabeth that the Anglican Church (Church of England) became firmly established and dominant. However, Elizabeth did her best to sort out the problem of religion.

Elizabeth wanted England to have peace and not be divided over religion. She tried to find ways which both the Catholic and Protestant sides would accept and be happy. She did not call herself the Head of the Church of England, instead she was known as the "Supreme Governor of the English Church".

Although Elizabeth insisted on protestant beliefs, she still allowed many things from the Catholic religion such as bishops, ordained priests, church decorations and priests' vestments. She also produced a prayer book in English, and allowed a Latin edition to be printed.

Elizabeth disliked and punished extreme Protestants and extreme Catholics who tried to convert people to their faiths. Church services were changed back to English. Although working for a compromise between different religious factions, she defended the fruit of the Reformation in essence.

The Church of England's doctrinal character today is largely the result of the Elizabethan Settlement, which sought to establish a comprehensive middle way between Roman Catholicism and Protestantism. While embracing some themes of the Protestant Reformation, the Church of England also maintains Catholic traditions of the ancient church and teachings of the Church Fathers. The Church of England has, as one of its distinguishing marks, a breadth and "open-mindedness". This tolerance has allowed Anglicans who emphasize the Catholic tradition and others who emphasize the Reformed tradition to coexist. Nowadays, the Church of England is the state church of England. The Archbishop of Canterbury is the most senior cleric, although the monarch is the supreme governor.

Ⅴ. Exercises

▶ **Multiple choices**: *Choose the best answer from the four choices given.*

1. According to the movie *Brideshead Revisited*, why does Lady Marchmain make it clear that Charles cannot marry Julia?
   A. Because Charles is of middle class while Julia was born to a noble family.
   B. Because Lady Marchmain strongly disapproves of his heavy drinking.
   C. Because Charles is an atheist(无神论者).
   D. Because Charles is a Canadian businessman.

2. *Brideshead Revisited* is a production of efforts from many countries except _____.
   A. the United Kingdom   B. Ireland
   C. Italy   D. Morocco

3. What is the direct cause for the Reformation?
   A. King Henry Ⅷ's effort to divorce his wife.
   B. King Henry Ⅷ's effort to break with Rome.
   C. King Henry Ⅷ's effort to support the Protestants.
   D. King Henry Ⅷ's effort to declare his supreme power over the church.

Unit Two　Religion

4. What is the main religion in Britain?

   A. Islam.　　　　　　　　　　　　B. Judaism.

   C. Christianity.　　　　　　　　　D. Hinduism.

5. Who is the "Supreme Governor of the Church of England"?

   A. The Pope.

   B. Prime Minister.

   C. The Archbishop of Canterbury.

   D. The British Monarch.

6. Which statement is NOT true about the Catholic Church?

   A. The Catholic Church is a denomination in Christianity.

   B. It is the largest denomination of Christians' in Britain.

   C. The Catholic Church is led by the Pope.

   D. The Catholic Church recognizes the Trinity.

7. Which is the most important sacrament of the Catholic Church?

   A. Baptism.　　　　　　　　　　　B. The Holy Eucharist.

   C. Confirmation.　　　　　　　　　D. The Holy Matrimony.

8. Which of the following statements is true?

   A. Nobles' demand for reform led to the period of history called the Reformation.

   B. England was a Protestant nation under the rule of Henry Ⅶ.

   C. King Edward Ⅵ issued *The Act of Supremacy* in 1534.

   D. Under Queen Elizabeth Ⅰ, England was a Protestant nation.

Blank-filling: *Fill in the blanks with the missing information.*

1. There are four composing parts in Britain, _____, _____, _____ and Northern Ireland. The official religion of England is _____. Most Christians belong to the _____ or the Church of Scotland. These are Protestant Churches. There are also many _____. _____ is the "Supreme Governor of the Church of England".

2. During the Middle Ages, _____ remained the dominant form of Western Christianity in Britain, but _____ became the independent established church in England and Wales in 1534 as a result of _____.

3. _____ refused to grant Henry Ⅷ a divorce from _____ who failed to produce a male heir, because the Roman Catholic faith believed in _____. It did not recognize, let alone support, divorce. King Henry Ⅷ issued _____ in 1534 and declared himself supreme head of _____. This marked the start of

centuries of religious conflict in Britain.

4. Like other Christians, Catholics believe _____ is a divine person, the Son of God. The Catholic Church also recognizes _____, i. e. that the Father, the Son and the Holy Spirit together are the only God. Some of the traditional worship practices of Roman Catholics include making the sign of _____, kneeling, bowing, and receiving _____ during their worship ceremonies. Their main form of worship is called the _____.

Translate & Appreciate: *Translate the classic lines from the movie into Chinese and share your understandings.*

1. Because, a camera is a mechanical device which records a moment in time, but not what that moment means or the emotions that it evokes. Whereas, a painting, however imperfect it may be, is an expression of… feeling, an expression of love. Not just a copy of something.

   _____
   _____
   _____
   _____

2. Just the place to bury a crock of gold. I should like to bury something precious; in every place I've been happy. And then when I was old, and ugly and miserable, I could come back, and dig it up, and remember.

   _____
   _____
   _____

3. If you asked me now who I am, the only answer I could give with any certainty would be my name: Charles Ryder. For the rest: my loves, my hates, down even to my deepest desires, I can no longer say whether these emotions are my own, or stolen from those I once so desperately wished to be. On second thoughts, one emotion remains my own. Alone among the borrowed and the second-hand, as pure as that faith from which I am still in flight: Guilt.

   _____
   _____
   _____
   _____

VI. Explore for More

The official religion of England is Christianity. Fill in the blanks and see whether you can have any findings.

Place of Origin	
Founder	
Sacred Text	
Christian Symbols	
Holy Places	
Major Festivals	
Main Branches (Denominations)	

Section B Se7en

> Ernest Hemingway once wrote, "The world is a fine place and worth fighting for." I agree with the second part.
>
> —Somerset in Se7en

 I. Warm-up Questions

1. What is the main religion in America?
2. Who were the early settlers in New England?
3. What are the seven deadly sins?

 II. Basics about the Movie

Genre: neo-noir, crime, thriller
Director: David Fincher
Starring: Brad Pitt
　　　　　Morgan Freeman
　　　　　Gwyneth Paltrow
Release Year: 1995
Running Time: 127 minutes
Country: the United States

 III. Synopsis

In an unnamed American city, soon-to-be-retiring detective William Somerset is partnered with short-tempered but idealistic David Mills, who has recently been transferred to the department, moving to the city with his wife Tracy. Mills introduces Somerset to

Unit Two Religion

Tracy, who is unhappy with the city and feels it is no place to raise a child. She discloses to Somerset that she is pregnant and has yet to inform her husband.

Somerset and Mills investigate a pair of murders. The first victim is an obese man forced to eat until his stomach ruptured. The second is a wealthy defense attorney who died from both fatal bloodletting and the removal of a pound of flesh. At each crime scene, the murderer leaves behind clues for the detectives, including the word *gluttony* at the obese man's home and *greed* at the attorney's office. Somerset recognizes them as part of the seven deadly sins and realizes the murders are related. The third victim is a known drug dealer and child molester. The word *sloth* is scrawled on the wall.

Somerset and Mills identify a man named John Doe, who flees when they go to his apartment. At Doe's apartment, they find hundreds of handwritten journals showing clues leading to a fourth victim. They arrive too late to prevent the death of the victim, a prostitute. They find *lust* written on the door. The fifth victim is a model, whose wall is written with the word *pride*.

Shortly after, as Somerset and Mills return to the police station, they are approached by a man covered in blood, surrendering himself. Mills recognizes him as Doe and arrests him. Doe, through his lawyer, advises there are two more victims and offers to take the detectives to them and confesses to all the murders.

The two detectives, following Doe's directions, drive him to a remote desert location. Within minutes, a delivery van approaches them and brings a box to them. Doe reveals that he was so jealous of Mills that he killed Tracy, her death being a result of his *envy*, and that her head is in the box. After Doe reveals that Tracy was pregnant, the furious Mills shoots Doe six times. Doe's death completes the seven sins.

IV. Culture Links

1. Religion in the United States

Religion in the United States is characterized by a diversity of religious beliefs and practices. Various religious faiths have flourished within the United States. A majority of Americans report that religion plays a very important role in their lives, a proportion unique among developed countries.

There are at least three reasons for the religious diversity in America. For one thing, the US Constitution guarantees every individual the right to practice his own religious belief. For another, American belief in individual freedom has been deeply rooted throughout its history. At last, as a nation of immigrants, the great diversity of ethnic backgrounds leads to the diversity of religious beliefs.

The majority of US adults are Christians, among which 46.5% are Protestants, and 20.8% profess Catholic belief. The same study says that other religions (including Judaism, Buddhism, Hinduism, and Islam) are practiced by about 6% of the population. According to a 2016 survey Mississippi is the most religious state in the country, while New Hampshire is the least religious state.

2. Protestantism in the United States

Protestantism is the largest group of Christians in the United States. It is a form of Christianity which originated with the Reformation. At the time of the Protestant Reformation, the Roman Catholic Church was the center of religious life in Western European countries. The Catholic pope and the priests played the role of parents to the people in spiritual matter.

The Protestants, on the other hand, insisted that all individuals must stand alone before God. If people sinned, they should seek forgiveness directly from God rather than from a priest. Protestants believe that every individual is solely responsible for his or her own relationship with God.

In England, a Protestant religion called Anglicans became the dominant force in social and political life. Some people in England, however, viewed religion differently. As a result, a new Protestant religion called Puritans (清教徒) evolved. The ruling Anglican church disapproved of Puritan beliefs and persecuted Puritans. Many Puritans fled England and came to America to escape religious persecution. So the early settlers in New England were Puritans.

Puritans believed in "original sin" and "predestination" (宿命论). They believed that all men were born sinners. The only way to be saved was by the grace of God. They believed that man must follow the Bible exactly because the Bible was a guide to all aspects of life including political, social and economic matters. Puritans followed a very simple life style and immersed themselves in their work. They made great contribution to art, sculpture, poetry, drama, economy, science and technology. Puritans lasted only a century or a little longer, but they have left the biggest stamp on American character and myth.

Along the way of development, various churches were free from governmental restriction or support, so one of the differences between American and European religious practice was that in the United States there was the separation of church and state early on its development. Therefore, the religion had no relevance for politics, education, and economic decisions.

3. Seven Deadly Sins

As the title of the film suggests, the main theme is sin and in particular, the seven deadly sins of gluttony, greed, sloth, lust, pride, envy and anger. These sins are believed in the Christian tradition to be deadly because they pose fatal obstacles to spiritual progress. The capital sins from lust to envy are generally associated with pride, which has been labeled as the father of all sins. The seven deadly sins have been described and elaborated upon in many works, including Chaucer's *Parson's Tale*, Dante's *Divine Comedy*, and *Summa Theologica* of Thomas Aquinas.

Gluttony is the over consumption of anything to the point of waste. Gluttony can be interpreted as selfishness which leads people to place concern with one's own interests above the well-being of others. Greed is a sin of desire. However, greed is always associated with the desire and pursuit of material possessions. Like pride, it can lead to not just some, but all evils. Sloth is defined as absence of interest or habitual disinclination to exertion. Lust is usually thought of as intense sexual desire, which leads to adultery, rape and other immoral sexual acts. However, lust could also mean simply desire in general; thus, lust for money, power, and other things is sinful. Anger can be defined as uncontrolled feelings of rage and hatred. Feelings of anger can lead to impatience, revenge, and self-destructive behavior, such as drug abuse or suicide. Envy, like greed and lust, is described as a sad or resentful eagerness towards the possession of someone else. The negative version of pride is considered the original and most serious of the seven deadly sins. It is also thought to be the source of the other capital sins.

V. Exercises

▸ **True or False Statements:** *Read the following statements and decide whether they are true (T) or false (F).*

　　　　　1. *Se7en* is an American neo-noir crime thriller film starring Brad Pitt, Morgan Freeman, etc.
　　　　　2. America is a nation where religion tends to be unitary.
　　　　　3. The main religion in America is Christianity. Most Christians are Protestants.

_____ 4. Protestantism is a form of Christianity which originated with the Reformation.

_____ 5. At the time of the Reformation, Protestant priests played the role of parents to the people in spiritual matter.

_____ 6. The Catholic Church believes that people should seek forgiveness directly from God rather than from a priest speaking in God's name.

_____ 7. Puritans fled England and came to America to escape religious persecution.

_____ 8. Puritans lasted only a century or a little longer, so they have left very small stamp on American character.

_____ 9. In America, there was the separation of church and state early on its development.

_____ 10. The capital sins from lust to envy are generally associated with gluttony, which has been labeled as the father of all sins.

- **Short-answer Questions**: *Give brief answers to the following questions.*

  1. What are the features of religion in the United States?
  _____
  _____

  2. Can you briefly summarize the fundamental beliefs of Puritans?
  _____
  _____

  3. Can you list out all the seven deadly sins?
  _____
  _____

- **Extracurricular Exploration**: *Explore the Internet. Find out the answers to the following questions and make a no-more-than-5-minute presentation.*

  1. What motifs(主题) and symbols can you detect in *Se7en*?

  2. Would it be true to say that *Se7en* is an unremittingly grim film(冷酷无情的电影)?

  3. Kevin Spacey, who plays John Doe in *Se7en*, has starred in other popular films such as *American Beauty* and *K-Pax*. What kind of roles does he play in these films?

Section C Noah

I. Movie Information (Explore and Find)

Genre: _____
Chinese Title: _____
Director: _____
Starring: _____
Running Time: _____ minutes
Release Year: 2014
Country: _____

> Use the information you have found to fill in the blanks.

Noah is a _____ (year) _____ (country) _____ (genre) film inspired by the Biblical story of _____ from the Book of _____.

The film stars as Noah, along with Jennifer Connelly, Emma Watson, etc. Noah's Ark is the vessel, which was built by _____ at the command to save himself, his family and the world's animals from a worldwide _____. The narrative features in a number of religions including _____, _____ and Islam.

II. Synopsis

As a young boy, Noah witnesses his father, Lamech, killed by a young Tubal-cain. Many years later, an adult Noah is living with his wife Naameh and their sons Shem, Ham, and Japheth. Haunted by dreams of a great flood, Noah goes to visit his grandfather Methuselah, who tells Noah that he was chosen for a reason.

With the help of fallen angels "Watchers", Noah and his family start to build an ark. After birds fly to the ark, Tubal-cain arrives with his followers and confronts Noah. Noah defies Tubal-cain and remarks that there is no escape for the line of Cain. Tubal-cain retreats and decides to build weapons to defeat the Watchers and take the ark. After the completion of the ark, animals of various species enter the ark and are put to sleep with incense.

After it starts raining, Tubal-cain becomes angry that he was not chosen to be saved and incites his followers to make a run for the ark. The Watchers hold off Tubal-cain and his followers as long as possible, sacrificing themselves to protect the ark.

Ila, the wife of Shem, discovers that she is pregnant as the rain stops and begs the Creator to let the child live. Noah believes that the ending of the rain implies that he must ensure the extinction of humans. Noah decides that, if the child is a girl, he will kill her. Months pass. Ila then gives birth to twin girls. In the meantime Ham has called Noah telling him the beasts are awake and eating each other. Tubal-cain emerges and attempts to hit Noah. Noah and Tubal-cain engage in combat. Tubal-cain forces Noah to the edge of the raft, but is eventually killed by Ham. Noah picks himself up and immediately goes to find Ila and the babies. On top of the ark, He finds Ila crying and telling him to wait to kill them until she can calm them down. Noah prepares to kill Ila's twins, but he spares them upon looking at his granddaughters and only feeling love.

Upon exiting the ark on the new land, a shameful Noah goes into isolation in a nearby cave, making wine to drown his sorrows. Having reconciled at the behest of Ila, Noah blesses the family as the beginning of a new human race and all witness an immense rainbow.

III. Culture Links

1. The Book of Genesis

The Book of Genesis is the first book of the Hebrew Bible and the Christian Old Testament.

The basic narrative expresses the central theme: God creates the world (along with creating the first man and woman) and appoints man as his regent(摄政者), but man proves disobedient and God exiles Adam and Eve  from the Garden of Eden. Then God destroys the world through the Flood. The new post-Flood world is also corrupt. God does not destroy it, instead calling one man, Abraham, to be the seed of its salvation(拯救). At God's command Abraham descends from his home into the land of Canaan, given to him by God, where he dwells as a sojourner(旅居者), along with his son Isaac and his grandson Jacob. Jacob's name is changed to Israel, and through the agency of his son Joseph, the children of Israel descend into Egypt, 70 people in all with their households. God promises them a future of greatness. Genesis ends with Israel in Egypt, ready for the coming of Moses and Exodus.

In Judaism, the importance of Genesis centers on the covenants(契约) linking God to his chosen people and the people to the Promised Land. Christianity has linked Genesis to certain Christian beliefs, primarily the need for salvation and the redemptive(赎罪) act of Christ on the Cross as the fulfillment of covenant promises as the Son of God.

2. Noah's Ark

Noah's Ark is the vessel, which, according to the Book of Genesis, was built by the Patriarch Noah at God's command to save himself, his family and the world's animals from a worldwide flood. The narrative features in a number of religions including Judaism, Christianity and Islam.

In the Book of Genesis, God sends a great flood to destroy the earth because of man's wickedness and because the earth is corrupt. God tells Noah, a righteous man in his generation, to build a large vessel to save his family and a representation of the world's animals. God gives detailed instructions for the Ark, and after its completion, sends the animals to Noah. God then sends the Flood which rises until all the mountains are covered and every living thing dies. Then "God remembered Noah," the waters abate, and dry land reappears. Noah, his family, and the animals leave the Ark.

The narrative has been elaborated in Judaism, Christianity and Islam. Although traditionally accepted as historical, biblical literalists continue to explore the region of the mountains of Ararat, in eastern Turkey, where the Bible says the Ark came to rest.

Ⅳ. Expansion

Explore the Internet. Find out meanings of the following idioms and phrases from the Bible and share the stories with the class.

1. Adam's apple

2. Achilles' heels

3. at the eleventh hour

4. make bricks without straw

5. cast pearls before swine

Ⅴ. Fun Time

The story of Noah building an ark to save his family and save thousands of animals from a flood which destroys all life on the earth is an epic from many people's childhood. It's a wonderful story, found in the Bible. But is it in fact, real history?

Now let's enjoy a history documentary published by BBC in 2003 and find out its theme and key points.

Theme: _____

Key points: _____

_____

_____

_____

Unit Three

Celebrities

Section A　The Iron Lady
Section B　Lincoln
Section C　The Social Network

Preface

There is a galaxy of great names in the history of Britain and the United States: William Shakespeare, Stephen Hawking, Thomas Edison, David Beckham, Michael Jordan, Oprah Winfrey, etc.

This unit highlights three celebrities predominantly from two areas—politics and business: Section A introduces a well-renowned female politician whose legends still remain although she passed away years ago; Section B illustrates a beloved statesman and renowned US ex-president, Abraham Lincoln; Section C is about a technical icon, a young billionaire who innovated the way people communicate, Mark Zuckerberg.

Unit Goals

- To have a deep understanding of the celebrities involved;
- To gain an insight into the causes of their success;
- To have a basic knowledge about the political systems in Britain and America.

Section A The Iron Lady

> Where there is discord, may we bring harmony; where there is error, may we bring truth;
>
> where there is doubt, may we bring faith; and where there is despair, may we bring hope.
>
> —Margaret Thatcher's 1979 election victory speech

 I. Warm-up Questions

1. Are there any women Prime Ministers or Presidents respectively in the history of the UK and the USA? If any, who are they?

2. Margaret Thatcher can be said to be one of the most influential political leaders in modern world. Who nicknamed Margaret Thatcher "the Iron Lady" and when?

3. What do you know about the British General Election and American Election?

 II. Basics about the Movie

Genre: biopic, drama
Director: Phyllida Lloyd
Starring: Meryl Streep
          Jim Broadbent
Release Year: 2011
Running Time: 104 minutes
Country: the UK, France

III. Synopsis

The movie adopts the flashback to review Margaret Thatcher's struggle from a girl of lower class origin to the first woman Prime Minister in British history. The elderly Margaret Thatcher is diagnosed with Alzheimer disease, and she refuses to accept the fact that her husband has died but finally manages to come to terms with his death. Old memories repeatedly come flooding back to her.

Young Margaret works in the grocery store her family opens and she is greatly inspired by her father's speech—"never go down with the crowds" "to go her own way". Her diligence and hard work earn her a place to Oxford. The degree from Oxford University serves as a good stepping stone to her future political career.

Upon graduation, Margaret plunges into politics but she meets her Waterloo at the age of 24 in running for a seat in Parliament, around which time she is dating with her future husband Denis Thatcher, a successful businessman and is proposed subsequently. Her political life becomes smooth after she gets married. She struggles to fit in as a "lady Member" of the House, to argue in the Cabinet as Education Secretary and makes up her mind to stand for Leader of the Conservative Party. She eventually makes it to be the first woman Prime Minister in history.

A chain of events during her time as Prime Minister are also examined in flashbacks, including rising unemployment related to her monetarist policies and the tight 1981 budget, the 1981 Brixton riot, the war with Argentina in 1982, the 1984—1985 UK miners' strike, and the bombing in Brighton of the Grand Hotel during the 1984 Conservative Party Conference.

The Iron Lady attempts to tell the story of Margaret Thatcher's life, from more than just a political standpoint, as she rises to become one of the most influential women in history.

IV. Culture Links

1. Margaret Thatcher (13 October 1925—8 April 2013)

Margaret Thatcher is the longest-serving British prime minister of the 20th century, and the first woman Member of Parliament and also the first woman to have held the office. She is nicknamed "the Iron Lady" to satire her but it later becomes a compliment.

Margaret Thatcher was born in a grocer's family in 1925. Much as depicted in the movie introduced above, young Margaret had an enthusiasm toward politics, especially the Conservative Party under the influence of her father. Margaret graduated from the renowned Oxford University, majoring in chemistry. Upon graduation, she became a research chemist before moving forward to be a barrier. She failed to get elected from 1950 to 1951 in succession, but she met her Mr. Right—Denis Thatcher, a successful and wealthy divorced businessman, who assisted Margaret with her political ambitions.

Margaret Thatcher was appointed Secretary of State for Education and Science in the early 1970s, and in 1975 she became the first woman Leader of the Opposition. Four years later, the Conservative Party won the General Election in 1979 and subsequently Margaret Thatcher became the Prime Minister. From then on, she won three General Elections in succession and had been the Prime Minister for eleven years and a half.

On moving into 10 Downing Street, the Thatcher government introduced a series of political and economic initiatives, including privatizing state-owned industries and promoting a more competitive spirit in the British economy. As to social welfare such as pension, unemployment benefits and child benefits was greatly curbed or even cut. Besides, the power and influence of trade unions was reduced. In this way, the inflation rate was brought under control and business profits increased, but the early 1980s saw the rapid rise in unemployment.

Thatcher's popularity during her first years in office waned amid recession and high unemployment, until victory in the 1982 Falklands War① and the recovering economy brought a resurgence of support, resulting in her decisive re-election in 1983. She narrowly escaped an assassination attempt in 1984, which was also reflected in the film.

In 1982 Margaret Thatcher visited Beijing and she menaced that the disastrous results might emerge if Chinese government intended to take back Hong Kong. Unfortunately, this time the Iron Lady met a tougher man Mr. Deng Xiaoping and she reluctantly signed the *Joint Declaration* in 1984, setting out with Chinese government an agreed mechanism by which the city would be returned to China in 1997.

Later on, the unpopular poll tax together with her reluctance to integrate the UK with the European Union rendered her government unwelcome and she resigned in 1990. In

---

① 1982年4月到6月间英国和阿根廷为争夺马尔维纳斯群岛(英国称福克兰群岛)的主权而爆发的一场战争,战争最终以英军获胜并重新占领该群岛而结束。

1992, she was given a life peerage as Baroness Thatcher which entitled her to sit in the House of Lords. In 2013, she died of a stroke in London at the age of 87. The Queen Elizabeth Ⅱ and her husband attended the funeral. The ceremonial funeral with military honors is one step down from a state funeral, which indicates her role in British people's minds.

Love her or hate her, there's no denying that Margaret Thatcher, "the Iron Lady", who had an incredible impact on British politics, has been lauded as one of the greatest and most influential politicians in British history.

2. British Political System

Modern Britain is a parliamentary democracy with a constitutional monarchy. The King or Queen is the head of the state, while virtually the most powerful leader is the Prime Minister, who is usually also the leader of the majority party winning the most seats in the General Election. As a parliamentary democracy, the British government is  characterized by a division of powers among three sects: the legislature, the executive and the judiciary.

The legislature in Britain is Parliament, which strictly comprises of the Crown, the House of Lords and the House of Commons. Palace of Westminster has become a metonymy for the UK Parliament. It is located on the northern bank of the River Thames, beside the Elizabeth Tower, or Big Ben. It has become a must-to-see tourist attraction for visitors. The Westminster system of government has also taken its name after it.

The Crown, namely the King or Queen has a symbolic, ceremonial and unpolitical role. The House of Lords, also known as the Upper House, currently consists of 700 or so life peers, 26 archbishops and bishops, 92 elected hereditary peers. Members of the House of Lords are appointed, not elected. The majority (about 700) of members are appointed for their lifetime by the Queen on the advice of the Prime Minister. Any British, Irish or Commonwealth citizen who is a UK resident and taxpayer over the age of 21 is eligible to be nominated or can apply to become a member, via the independent House of Lords Appointments Commission. The House of Lords is characterized by "independence of thought". This is partly because a significant part of the membership is non-party-political, for example, the Crossbenchers(中立议员) and bishops.

The House of Commons is also referred to as the Lower House. The UK public elects 650 Members of Parliament (MPs) to represent their interests and concerns in the House of Commons. MPs consider and propose new laws, and can scrutinize government policies by asking ministers questions about current issues either in the Commons Chamber or in Committees. Besides, they can influence future government policy.

The executive refers to the government, which constitutes the Prime Minister (PM), the Cabinet ministers and assistants to the ministers. In the UK, the Prime Minister leads the government with the support of the Cabinet and ministers. The Prime Minister is appointed by the Sovereign. Ministers are chosen by the Prime Minister from the members of the House of Commons and House of Lords and they are appointed by the Sovereign on the advice of the Prime Minister.

The Cabinet is the core of the British political system. The Cabinet is made up of the senior members of government. Every week during Parliament, members of the Cabinet (Secretaries of State from all departments and some other ministers) meet at 10 Downing Street to discuss the most important issues for the government.

Apart from the Central government, there are also devolved government and local government: In Scotland, Wales and Northern Ireland, devolved administrations are responsible for many domestic policy issues, and their Parliaments/Assemblies have law-making powers for those areas. The Scottish Government, Welsh Government, and the Northern Ireland Executive are responsible for such aspects as health, education, culture, environment, transport, etc. Apart from devolved government, many parts of England have 2 tiers of local government: county councils and district, borough or city councils. In some parts of the country, there's just one tier of local government providing all the functions, known as a "unitary authority". This can be a city, borough or county council—or it may just be called "council". As well as these, many areas also have parish or town councils.

The judiciary of the United Kingdom embraces the separate judiciaries of the three legal systems in England and Wales, Northern Ireland and Scotland, which makes it rather complicated. The Supreme Court is a relatively new Court established in October 2009 in the wake of the *Constitutional Reform Act* of 2005. It is headed

by the President and Deputy President of the Supreme Court and is composed of a further ten Justices of the Supreme Court. The Justices do not wear any gowns or wigs in court, but on ceremonial occasions they wear black damask gowns with gold lace without a wig.

General Election of Britain is to be held on the first Thursday in May every five years and the Prime Minister can call a **snap election**(提前选举) when the government loses a confidence motion or when a two-thirds supermajority of MPs vote in favor in accordance with *Fixed Term Parliaments Act* (2011). The nearest snap election took place on 8 June, 2017 as the Prime Minister Theresa May announced on April 18. British General Election differs from the one in the USA in that it does not result in a Prime Minister directly; instead, it leads to a winning party. The Leader of the winning party will take on the position.

* * *

Dissolution of Parliament (解散议会)

By law, Parliament is dissolved 25 working days before a General Election. When Parliament is dissolved, every seat in the House of Commons becomes vacant. All business in the House comes to an end. There are no Members of Parliament. MPs revert to being members of the public and lose privileges associated with being a Member of Parliament. Until a new Parliament is elected, there are no MPs. Those who wish to be MPs again must stand again as candidates for election.

Parliament and Government are two separate institutions. Government does not resign when Parliament is dissolved. Government ministers remain in charge of their departments until after the result of the election is known and a new administration is formed.

* * *

Hung Parliament (悬浮议会)

When a general election results in no single political party winning an overall majority,

it is known as a **hung Parliament**. As it can be seen in the 2017 General Election, of all the 650 seats the ruling Conservative Party wins 318, and the biggest Opposition—the Labor Party wins 262, neither of them have seats more than 326, hence the parliament can be called hung. In this condition, the Prime Minister can choose to form a coalition or a minority government.

* * *

Shadow Cabinet（影子内阁）

The **Shadow Cabinet** is a feature of the Westminster system of government. It consists of a senior group of opposition spokespeople who, under the leadership of the Leader of the Opposition, form an alternative cabinet to that of the government, and whose members *shadow* or mirror the positions of each individual member of the Cabinet. Members of a shadow cabinet are often but not always appointed to a Cabinet post if and when their party gets into government. It is the Shadow Cabinet's responsibility to criticise the policies and actions of the government, as well to offer an alternative program.

3. British Political Parties

Before the mid-19th century politics in the United Kingdom was dominated by the Whigs and the Tories. By the mid 19th century the Tories had evolved into the Conservative Party, and the Whigs had evolved into the Liberal Party. The Liberals and Conservatives dominated the political scene until the 1920s, when the Liberal Party declined in popularity and suffered a long stream of resignations. It was replaced as the main anti-Tory opposition party by the newly emerging Labour Party. Since then the Conservative and Labour parties have dominated British politics, and have alternated in government ever since.

In modern Britain, there are top two biggest parties: the Conservative and the Labor. Others also include the Democratic Liberal, Scottish National Party, Green Party, etc.

The **Conservative Party**, officially called the Conservative and Unionist Party, is a centre-right political party in the United Kingdom. The Conservative Party's platform involves support for free market capitalism, free enterprise, fiscal conservatism, a strong national defence, deregulation, and restrictions on trade unions. Conservative Prime Ministers led governments for 57 years of the twentieth century, including Winston Churchill (1940—1945, 1951—1955) and Margaret Thatcher (1979—1990). The Conservative Party's domination of British politics throughout the twentieth century has led to them being referred to as one of the most successful political parties in the Western world. Blue is usually associated with conservative parties, originating from its use by the Tory party in the United Kingdom; thus, blue is the colour for the Conservative Party.

Unit Three Celebrities

The **Labour Party** is a centre-left political party in the United Kingdom. After its foundation in 1900, the Labour Party overtook the Liberal Party as the main opposition to the Conservative Party in the early 1920s. It believes in an egalitarian economy and "redistributive" function of the government—to transfer wealth from the rich to the poor by means of imposing heavy taxes on the affluent ones. The most influential Labour government is the one in 1945, which set up the National Health Service to provide high-quality, free health care for all. The colour red symbolises left-wing ideologies in many countries, and Britain is no exception: Labour has long been identified with red, a political colour traditionally affiliated with socialism and the labour movement.

 Ⅴ. **Exercises**

Multiple Choices: *Choose the best answer from the four choices given.*

1. Which of the following has never been the Prime Minister of Britain?
    A. Winston Churchill.   B. Tony Blair.
    C. Harold Wilson.   D. Thomas Jefferson.
2. Which of the following issues is not connected with Margaret Thatcher?
    A. Negotiation of Hong Kong Hand-over.
    B. Privatization of state-owned industries.
    C. Large-scale unemployment.
    D. Rising social welfare.
3. Which of the following statements is NOT true about the British political system?
    A. The United Kingdom adopts the tripartite political system.
    B. Conventionally, the General Election is held every five years.
    C. The Prime Minister is the head of the country.
    D. The Parliament is mainly responsible for law-making.
4. Which of the following is not a sect of the British legislature?
    A. The King or Queen.   B. The Prime Minister.
    C. The House of Lords.   D. The House of Commons.
5. Which is true about the British Prime Minister?
    A. The Prime Minister must be chosen in the General Election.
    B. The Prime Minister has the right to dissolve the Parliament.
    C. The Prime Minster can take on the position for more than two terms.
    D. The Prime Minister is not necessarily the leader of the winning party.

6. Compared with the US counterparts, which of the following cannot be described as British characteristics?

  A. The Shadow Cabinet.   B. Separation of the three powers.
  C. The Hung Parliament.   D. Empowering from the Crown.

▶ **Blank-filling**: *Fill in the blanks with the missing information.*

1. Margaret Thatcher is the _____ woman Prime Minister in British history. The year 2016 witnessed the first woman PM in the 21st century, _____.

2. Margaret Thatcher wins the General Election for _____ times and she serves the Prime Minister from the year _____ to _____. _____ is the youngest PM in British history now; before him, this record was kept by _____. The three PMs mentioned above all graduated from the same University, _____ University.

3. The UK is a constitutional monarchy country; the _____ or _____ is the head of the country. The role of the monarch is _____, _____, and _____ while the most powerful person undoubtedly is the _____.

4. The British government is characterized by a division of powers among three sects: the _____, the _____, and the _____.

5. The biggest political parties in modern Britain is _____ and _____. British General Election is supposed to be held every _____ years.

▶ **Translate & Appreciate**: *Translate the classic lines from the movie into Chinese and share your understandings.*

1. One's life must matter. Beyond the cooking and the cleaning and the children, one's life must mean more than that. I cannot die washing up a tea cup.

  _____
  _____

2. Give people the freedom and opportunity to fulfill their own potential, especially the young. There's no good pretending we're all equal, we are not all the same. Never have been, never will be. We should encourage our children to aspire to achieve more than we have, for our children today will be the leaders of tomorrow.

  _____
  _____
  _____
  _____

Unit Three   Celebrities

3. Watch your thoughts, for they become words.
   Watch your words, for they become your actions.
   Watch your actions, for they become habits.
   Watch your habits, for they become your character.
   And watch your character, for it becomes your destiny.
   What we think, we become.

   _____
   _____
   _____
   _____

▶ **Voice Your Opinion**: *Read the following tit-for-tat reviews about The Iron Lady and voice your opinions on this movie after you finish watching it.*

⟨1⟩

By Edwina Currie (Junior Health Minister under Thatcher)

Towering above everything else in this wonderful movie is the magnificent performance of Meryl Streep, whose majestic portrayal of Margaret Thatcher in *The Iron Lady* confirms that she is the greatest screen actress of modern times.

What is so outstanding is how she captures the essence of Margaret's personality, right down to the curl of her lip. This is no mere imitation. It shows what Margaret was really like. Streep's screen character embodies Margaret's steely determination, overlaying a considerable sense of insecurity.

As the film so powerfully reveals, that insecurity was bred from the feeling of being an outsider in Tory politics—not only as a woman in a male-dominated world, but also as the daughter of a Lincolnshire shopkeeper.

As a female politician hailing from the same kind of background, brought up in a northern household with a father who ran a small business, I always strongly identified with Margaret and empathized with her battles against the patriarchal establishment.

Throughout the film, which is released next month, the image of Margaret in the kitchen washing up the teacups is used to highlight the sexism she had to endure.

There are also several vivid scenes that expose the sneering contempt that the traditional elite had towards her. An example is during the Falklands conflict, when she is faced with barbs that, because of her gender, she is clueless about war.

Such condescension is dramatically overcome with her heroic leadership. Another is a stunning visual moment, shot from above, when she enters the Commons and appears as a lone figure in a pale outfit amid a sea of dark, masculine suits.

One of the most poignant moments is when she learns that she has won a place to study at Oxford University, thereby beginning the journey to the very top of politics. It was difficult to watch her joy without feeling a lump in my throat.

I have a few gripes, however. Streep hasn't quite got right Margaret's style of walking. She is too stately, too controlled, whereas Margaret had a kind of quick scuttle—desperate to get to the next meeting.

I also found excessive the film's emphasis on her decline in old age. I could have done with far less of Margaret losing her mind. At times, it was both insensitive and irrelevant.

In some places, the chronology goes awry—so the Falklands war follows the miners' strike and the major series of privatizations, whereas the reality was the other way round. It was the victory over Argentina that gave Margaret the confidence to take on the unions.

Also, I wonder why the film's producers made her a blonde whereas, in truth, she was a natural brunette. The transformation to blonde locks was part of her image make-over, and could have been turned into an interesting part of the drama.

But these are only minor quibbles; I cannot recommend this film more highly. It is a worthy tribute to one of our greatest Prime Ministers.

Key points: _____

_____

_____

_____

⟨2⟩

By Simon Heffer

There was a genre of film popular in the seventies' America called the "exploitation movie". It was so-called because it exploited sensational, lurid or morbid themes for the gratification of its audience. All films are, by their nature, voyeuristic, but these were repellently so.

It was an unsavoury genre and, like all fads, it eventually had its day. However, it has returned spectacularly in this film.

It became clear several years ago that Lady Thatcher had been officially dehumanised. She is sometimes written about in tones that suggest she is a criminal on a par with

Unit Three Celebrities

Hitler. Even today, mentioning her name on tiresome Radio 4 "comedy" programmes is a reliable means for some scrofulous little creep posing as a comedian to get a laugh.

There are websites that claim to be organising parties to celebrate her death. In short, she is treated by large sections of the media, and by a comparatively smaller section of society, as though she deserves nothing but contempt and obloquy for her defeat of socialism. The film pretends to be more nuanced about her. Meryl Streep, even claims to believe she has done Lady Thatcher a favour. She certainly does a remarkably convincing impersonation of her and, if they give Oscars for mimicry, she will doubtlessly win one.

However, the portrayal of Lady Thatcher as a demented old lady, while she still lives and tries to cope with the debilitating illnesses of old age, is simply cruel.

It is deeply intrusive—and the ultimate testament to the "creative" world's acceptance, and exploitation, of her dehumanization.

Lady Thatcher in her heyday was a far more subtle character than she appears in this film, whose screenwriter seems to have swallowed every cliché and prejudice about our greatest living stateswoman.

I found the film profoundly upsetting, mainly because of its invasion of Lady Thatcher's privacy, but also because of its reminder that we refuse to accept the greatness of the woman and her achievements.

History will be kinder to her than it will to third-rate attempts to represent her in films such as this.

Key points: _____
_____
_____
_____

Do some research to verify the reliability of the movie in depicting Margaret Thatcher before you put down your ideas.

Your opinion: _____
_____
_____
_____

Section B Lincoln

> ... and that government of the people, by the people, for the people, shall not perish from the earth.
>
> —Abraham Lincoln

 I. Warm-up Questions

1. What do you think about Abraham Lincoln?

2. How much do you know about the American Civil War? When and why did the war break out?

3. Lincoln is listed on the top two of the most popular presidents of the United States. Do you know why?

 II. Basics about the Movie

Genre: biography, drama, history
Director: Steven Spielberg
Starring: Daniel Day-Lewis
Running Time: 150 minutes
Release Year: 2012
Country: the United States

 III. Synopsis

Lincoln is a 2012 historical drama film, which primarily covers Lincoln's final four months from late 1864 to early 1865, focusing on his efforts in January 1865 to have the *Thirteenth Amendment* to the *United States Constitution* passed. The movie both wins wide

Unit Three Celebrities

critical acclaim and commercial success.

With the defeat of the Confederate States, the Civil War is expected to come to an end soon. In January 1865, President Abraham Lincoln worries that his war-time 1863 *Emancipation Proclamation* may be discarded once the war is over and that the proposed Thirteenth Amendment will be defeated. He feels it imperative to pass the amendment so that those freed slaves will not be re-enslaved while the ultimate passage of the amendment needs the support of both Republicans and Democrats. Some of his advisors suggest that he should wait for a better timing, but Lincoln cannot wait and he is intent on readmitting the southern states into the Union.

Lincoln relies heavily on the support of an influential founder of the Republic Party, Francis Preston Blair, who has two sons in the army and therefore is keen to end the hostilities between the North and the South. Realizing he cannot afford to lose Blair's help, Lincoln makes compromises and authorizes Blair's mission to engage the Confederate government in peace negotiation first with much reluctance. Meanwhile, Lincoln doesn't give up his efforts. Together with the Secretary of State, Lincoln tries every means to win the votes, including offering federal jobs as an exchange. But to make things worse, the news about the coming of Confederate envoys and their mission circulate. Both Democrats and Republicans intend to advocate postponing the vote on the amendment, but Lincoln insists. Finally, the vote is passed by a narrow margin.

In the subsequent events, Lincoln declares slavery cannot be restored. On April 3 Lincoln meets with Lieutenant General Ulysses S. Grant, who, six days later, accepts the surrender of General Robert E. Lee. On April 14, Lincoln is in a meeting when he is reminded that his wife is waiting to take them to their evening at Ford's Theatre. …

Ⅳ. Culture Links

1. The American Civil War (1861—1865)

The American Civil War is also referred to as the War Between the States. It began on April 12, 1861 when Confederate General opened fire on Fort Sumter, South Carolina and lasted until May 26, 1865.

Many factors contributed to the outbreak of the Civil War, of which the most fundamental and immediate cause was slavery. Slavery had existed since the first blacks were brought onto the North American Continent. In the South, the land was abundant, fertile and suitable for planting crops, especially cotton; the planters depended heavily on the labor of black slaves to manage the plantation and support their economy. In other words, without black slaves the Southern economy would collapse. In the North, there existed an increasing demand for labor to work in factories, so the Northerners supported the abolition of slavery with an eye to getting more slave labor to develop their burgeoning industry.

Other causes also included economic and social factors. Due to the divergence in social, economic and political viewpoints, the South and the North drifted apart from each other gradually. They struggled to keep the Union together until in 1860 Abraham Lincoln was elected as the 16th President. Lincoln was deemed as an active advocate to abolish slavery; therefore, his success in election became the fuse of the war. Besides, political divergence partly accounted for the final outbreak of the war.

The turning point of the war was in July 1863 at Gettysburg, where the Union army defeated the Confederate army. In April 1865, General Robert Lee surrendered to General Grant of the Union army, so did all the other Confederate troops very soon. The American Civil War was America's bloodiest clash and it resulted in the deaths of more than 620,000 with millions more injured.

2. Abraham Lincoln (February 12, 1809—April 15, 1865)

Abraham Lincoln, the son of a Kentucky frontiersman, became one of the most respectable presidents of the United States after his struggle from a self-taught lawyer to a legislator and vocal opponent of slavery.

Lincoln was born on February 12, 1809 in Kentucky. His family moved to southern Indiana in 1816 and Illinois in 1930. Lincoln's formal schooling was limited to three brief periods in local schools, as he had to work constantly to support his family. He first worked on a river flatboat, then worked as a shopkeeper and a postmaster in Illinois, where he studied law on his own and became a lawyer.

Lincoln married Mary Todd on November 4, 1842 and they had four sons—Robert, Edward, William and Thomas. Unfortunately, three of them died before they grew up; Robert was the only child to live to adulthood and have children. Mary Todd Lincoln lost her mind after the successive deaths of her three sons and husband.

In 1858 Lincoln ran against Stephen A. Douglas for Senator. He lost the election, but in debating with Douglas he gained a national reputation that won him the Republican nomination for President in 1860. In November 1860 shortly before the outbreak of the Civil War, Lincoln was elected the 16th president of the United States.

Lincoln proved to be a shrewd military strategist and a savvy leader: His *Emancipation Proclamation* paved the way for slavery's abolition, while his Gettysburg Address stands as one of the most famous pieces of oratory in American history. In April 1865, with the Union on the brink of victory, Abraham Lincoln was assassinated by the Confederate sympathizer John Wilkes Booth; his untimely death made him a martyr to the cause of liberty, and he is widely regarded as one of the greatest presidents in US history.

3. Gettysburg Address

Gettysburg Address is one of the best-known speeches in American history, a speech delivered by Abraham Lincoln on November 19, 1863, at the dedication of the Soldiers' National Cemetery in Gettysburg, Pennsylvania, four and a half months after the Union armies defeated those of the Confederacy at the Battle of Gettysburg.

This 272-word address became the most quoted speech in American history. It goes like this:

Four score and seven years ago our fathers brought forth on this continent, a new nation, conceived in Liberty, and dedicated to the proposition that all men are created equal.

Now we are engaged in a great civil war, testing whether that nation, or any nation so conceived and so dedicated, can long endure. We are met on a great battle-field of that war. We have come to dedicate a portion of that field, as a final resting-place for those who here gave their lives that that nation might live. It is altogether fitting and proper that we should do this.

But, in a larger sense, we cannot dedicate—we cannot consecrate—we cannot hallow—this ground. The brave men, living and dead, who struggled here, have consecrated it far above our poor power to add or detract. The world will little note, nor long remember what we say here, but it can never forget what they did here. It is for us the living, rather, to be dedicated here to the unfinished work which they who fought here have thus far so nobly advanced. It is rather for us to be here dedicated to the great task remaining before us—that from these honored dead we take increased devotion to that cause for which they gave the last full measure of devotion—that we here highly resolve that these dead shall not have died in vain—that this nation, under God, shall have a new birth of freedom—and that government of the people, by the people, for the people, shall not perish from the earth.

4. American Political System

The United States of America is a federal constitutional republic country with 50 states and a federal district. It is run under the guideline of *The Constitution of the United States*, which was drawn up in 1787 and came into effect in 1789. The most striking characteristics of the Constitution is "checks and balances" (三权分立) and the specification of the respective powers of the federal government and the state government wherein.

The Legislature in America resides in the Congress, the chief function of which is to pass laws for the Union. The Congress consists of two houses: the Senate and the House of Representatives. **Senates** are chosen directly in their state and can serve a 6-year term unlimitedly if they have the honor of repeated reelection. Each state has two Senates, hence there are all together 100 voting members in all. **The House of Representatives** is larger in number, all together 435 voting numbers divided among the 50 states according to their total population. Besides, there are also 6 non-voting representatives from Puerto Rico, the District of Columbia and four other territories of the US.

The Executive is composed of 15 departments and various independent agencies. The US. President is the head of the Executive and the Cabinet(内阁) provides chief source of advice and assistance to the President. The President has enormous powers: he can manage national affairs and the working of the federal government; he can control American foreign policy; he can exert influence on law-making; he can even influence the decision of the federal court. The Cabinet is made up of the heads of the 15 executive departments and is the nucleus(核心) of leadership.

The Judiciary constitutes three-tier courts: the Supreme Court, the courts of appeals and the district courts. **The Supreme Court** is the highest court and all its members are appointed by the President and the Senate's approval. There are 12 courts of appeals all over the country and they are supposed to share the burden of the Supreme Court. Besides, there are 94 district courts, the lowest unit of the federal judicial system across the country. On top of the federal judicial system, each state has its own judicial system, court of law, a police force and a prison system. What is noteworthy about the US Judiciary is that all American courts use the jury system and common law.

5. American Political Parties & Election

America adopts the two-party system and the two major parties are the Democratic Party and the Republic Party. The name of **the Democratic Party** can be traced back to the

Unit Three Celebrities

1830s and it is historically the party of labor, minorities and progressive reformers. **The Republic Party** originated from a party of northern slavery-opposing capitalists in 1854. Comparatively speaking, the Democratic Party holds a liberal ideology while the Republic Party is said to be more conservative. Their differences can be mirrored in their attitudes toward economic issues, social issues and foreign affairs, etc.

American Presidential Election takes place every 4 years. The US general election is normally divided into two stages. During the first stage, each state will have to choose presidential electors according to the number of its Representatives and Senators in the Congress. All those 538 presidential electors compose the United States Electoral College (总统选举团). The second stage is a matter of form as each elector will choose his or her party nominees as the future president. American election is to be held on the second Tuesday in November and on the January 20 of next year, the newly-elected president will make an inauguration speech.

V. Exercises

- **True or False Statements**: *Read the following statements and decide whether they are true (T) or false (F).*

    _____ 1. The movie *Lincoln* reviews the whole life story of Abraham Lincoln.

    _____ 2. Abraham Lincoln was a Democrat President who won the election twice.

    _____ 3. The American Civil War lasted for 8 years, during which the *Emancipation Proclamation* was issued.

    _____ 4. Lincoln was the leader of the Confederate, and he defeated General Lee and his forces.

    _____ 5. The Gettysburg Battle was the turning point of the Civil War.

    _____ 6. Lincoln knew the significance of the Gettysburg Battle, so he delivered his world-famous address to encourage his soldiers to keep up high morale.

    _____ 7. Slavery is the direct and sole cause of American Civil War.

    _____ 8. Abraham Lincoln is permanently missed by the American people for his contribution to the unification of the nation and his sacrifice to the liberation of black slaves.

    _____ 9. US president is both the head and the most powerful person in the country.

    _____ 10. The power of the American president is so enormous that no one can actually check him.

- **Short-answer Questions**: *Give brief answers to the following questions.*

    1. When did the American Civil War begin and end?

    2. What are the causes of the American Civil War?

    3. What are Lincoln's chief achievements?

    4. What if the American Civil War hadn't happened?

- **Extracurricular Exploration**: *Explore the Internet. Find out the answers to the following questions and make a no-more-than-5-minute presentation.*

    1. Surf the Internet. Find more anecdotes about Lincoln and share them with the class.

    2. Watch the movie *Lincoln* to find whether there are any discrepancies between history and the movie?

    3. Compare the political system and the major parties between the UK and the USA.

Unit Three Celebrities

Section C   The Social Network

Ⅰ. Movie Information（Explore and Find）

Genre: _____
Chinese Title: _____
Director: _____
Starring: _____
Running Time: 120 minutes
Release Year: _____
Country: _____

▸ Use the information you have found to fill in the blanks.

The Social Network is a _____（year）_____（country）_____（genre）film directed by _____ and written by Aaron Sorkin. Adapted from Ben Mezrich's 2009 book *The Accidental Billionaires*: *The Founding of Facebook, A Tale of Sex, Money, Genius, and Betrayal*, the film portrays the founding of social networking website _____ and the resulting lawsuits. It stars _____ as founder Mark Zuckerberg, along with _____ as Eduardo Saverin, _____ as Sean Parker, and _____ as Cameron and Tyler Winklevoss. Neither Zuckerberg nor any other Facebook staff were involved with the project, although Saverin was a consultant for Mezrich's book. The film was released in the United States by _____（distributing company）on October 1, 2010.

At the 83rd Academy Awards, the film received _____ nominations, including Best Picture, Best Director for Fincher, and Best Actor for Eisenberg, and won three for _____, _____, and _____. The film also received awards for Best Motion Picture—Drama, Best Director, Best Screenplay, and Best Original Score at the 68th Golden Globe Awards.

Ⅱ. Synopsis

In October 2003, Mark Zuckerberg breaks up with his girlfriend Erica Albright. Zuckerberg is so depressed that he writes an insulting entry about Albright on his blog and then by hacking into college databases and stealing photos, he creates a campus website called Facemash which allows web visitors to rate their beauty. When it is found out, Zuckerberg is given an academic probation as long as six months.

The accidental popularity of Facemash attracts the attention of twin brothers and their business partner. They ask Zuckerberg in to work on a social network which mainly features the exclusive nature of Harvard students and aims at dating and Zuckerberg says yes. Later on, Zuckerberg decides to work for his idea of another social networking website *Thefacebook* exclusive to Ivy League students. And his friend Saverin provides the initial funding and it hits off. As *Thefacebook* grows in popularity, Zuckerberg extends the network to other Ivy Leagues such as Yale University, Columbia University and Stanford University.

Zuckerberg soon finds him in two lawsuits: one is charged by the twin brothers while the other is from his friend and sponsor Eduardo Saverin. When hearing of *Thefacebook*, the Winklevoss twins and Narendra are incensed, believing that Zuckerberg stole their idea while keeping them deliberately in the dark by stalling on developing the Harvard Connection website. They raise their complaint with Harvard President. Meanwhile, Saverin objects to Parker making business decisions for Facebook and freezes the company's bank account in the resulting dispute. He later relents when Zuckerberg reveals that they have secured $500,000 from angel investor Peter Thiel. However, Saverin becomes enraged when he discovers that the new investment deal allows his share of Facebook to be diluted from 34% to 0.03%, while maintaining the ownership percentage of all other parties.

The epilogue states that Cameron and Tyler Winklevoss received a settlement of $65 million, signed a non-disclosure agreement, and rowed in the 2008 Beijing Olympics, placing sixth; Eduardo Saverin received a settlement of an unknown amount and his name was restored to the Facebook masthead as a co-founder; the website has over 500 million members in 207 countries and is valued at 25 billion dollars; and eventually Mark Zuckerberg is the world's youngest billionaire.

Unit Three   Celebrities

 III. Culture Links

In this movie, Zuckerberg and his friends set up *Facebook* in the dorm of Harvard University. Let's know something more about his partners in real life. Supply the missing information.

▶ 1. Mark Zuckerberg

Date of birth: May 14, _____
Title: Co-founder, Chairman & CEO of Facebook
Source of Wealth: Facebook, Self Made
Residence: _____, California
Citizenship: the United States
Marital Status: Married
Spouse: _____
Children: two daughters
Education: _____, Harvard University

▶ 2. Eduardo Saverin

Date of birth: 19 March, _____
Occupation: a _____—born Internet entrepreneur and angel investor; co-founder of Facebook
Residence: Singapore
Citizenship: _____
Marital Status: Married
Education: Harvard University

▶ 3. Andrew McCollum

Date of birth: Unknown
Citizenship: _____
Title: Co-founder of Facebook
Residence: Unknown
Education: A. B. in _____
　　　　　　 Ed. M. in _____
　　　　　　 Harvard University

英美经典影视与文化教程
Anglo-American Classic Movies and Culture

 IV. **Expansion**

Previously, Mark Zuckerberg is often compared with Bill Gates due to the fact that they share a bunch of similarities. In 2014, Evan Spiegel took the place of Mark Zuckerberg as the youngest billionaire. Can you assort them out and finish the table?

Date of birth			
Spouse			
Children			
Residence			
Nationality			
Source of Wealth			
Education			
Language			
Wealth			
Charity			

 V. **Fun Time**

Watch the speech Zuckerberg delivered on the Commencement of Harvard University in May, 2017 and especially pay attention to what he mocks about *The Social Network*.

Unit Four

Holidays

Section A   Love Actually
Section B   Groundhog Day
Section C   Rise of the Guardians

Preface

In English, the word "holiday" evolves from "holy day"; therefore, it is not difficult to find that most of the festivals or holidays have religious beginnings, particularly Christianity in the Western countries. Festivals and holidays are a good window to learn an alien country's history, traditions and beliefs.

In this unit, we are going to have a closer look at the Western holidays—How did they originate? How do local people celebrate them? What are the common symbols for them? In the wake of social advance and globalization, will the Western holidays take the place of some traditional holidays in underdeveloped areas and countries?

Unit Goals

- To get a general knowledge of the British and American festivals;
- To learn how local people observe their festivals;
- To make a comparison between Chinese festivals and Western ones.

Section A Love Actually

> If all the year were playing holidays, to sport would be as tedious as to work.
>
> —William Shakespeare

I. Warm-up Questions

1. How many Western holidays do you know? Arrange them according to time sequence.
2. Which holiday is the most important in the Western world? What is its origin?
3. What's your favorite holiday and why?

II. Basics about the Movie

Genre: romance, comedy
Director: Richard Curtis
Starring: Hugh Grant, Keira Knightley, Emma Thompson, Colin Firth, etc
Release Year: 2003
Running Time: 136 minutes
Country: the UK, the US, France

III. Synopsis

Love Actually is a 2003 Christmas-themed romantic comedy film. It features an ensemble cast and many Britain's famous actors and actresses are on the list. All the stories in the movie happen several weeks before Christmas and the plots advance on the weekly basis. An epilogue of what happens one month after Christmas is also included.

The movie tells a collection of seemingly interdependent stories of the same theme—love, love of all kinds, including the love between husband and wife, stepfather and stepson, mother and daughter, boyfriend and girlfriend... And actually those stories are intertwined in one way or another.

Love buds between the newly-elected Prime Minister David and the new household staff Natalie; the delicate feeling emerges between the newly-wedded couple Juliet, Peter, and the best man Mark; writer Jamie meets his Portugal housekeeper after an unexpected betrayal, and they become deadly attracted to each other even without the help of communication via language; there exists a love triangle between the managing director Harry, his wife Karen, and his secretary Mia; an affectionate husband mourns over the death of his wife Joanna and meanwhile he finds his 10-year-old stepson Sam is obsessed with an American girl, coincidentally enough, by the name of Joanna, who is going to return to the USA; a British young man Colin flies to Wisconsin, America to seek romance and there he meets four attractive women; an American girl Sarah harbors secret love for Karl, the creative designer of the same company and they are going to move forward while Sarah's mentally ill brother always needs her at critical moments; professional body doubles for films John and Judy click immediately even for embarrassing scenes and they decide to get serious in relationship.

The movie also tells stories about several others: a rock and roll legend Billy Mack who tries to record a Christmas song adapted from the classic song *Love is All Around*, and during the season his new song resounds everywhere and he finds his deep affection for his chubby manager Joe. Rufus, a salesman obsessed with gift-wrapping, is also a thread in the movie.

The movie is permeated with Christmas atmosphere and love all around.

IV. Culture Links

1. Religious Holidays in the UK

In Britain or even in the Western world, many holidays have their origins in religion, especially in Christianity, such as Christmas, Easter, and Boxing Day.

Christmas falls on the 25th of December and the celebrations begin from Christmas

Eve and last till after the New Year. The true origin of Christmas is filled with controversy. Legend has it that the commencement of Christmas lies in pagan worship(Mithraism,密特拉教) long before the introduction of Christianity. Today, Christians deem Christmas as the celebration of the birth of Jesus Christ. Christmas has come down to people as a day of thanksgiving and rejoicing—a day of good cheer and goodwill to others and it is the most significant festival in many Western countries. A Christmas is not perfect without a dinner featured with turkeys, decoration of Christmas trees, gifts and greetings. On Christmas Eve, Santa Claus is expected to deliver gifts in the stockings hung on the bed of good children.

Easter is the oldest Christian holiday and the most important day of the church year. It is the holiday that celebrates and commemorates the resurrection(耶稣复活) of Jesus Christ three days after his death. Unlike Christmas, Easter and its holiday are not on fixed days. They are called moveable feasts because Easter Sunday can fall anywhere between March 22 and April 25, always celebrated on the first Sunday following the first full moon after the spring equinox(春分).

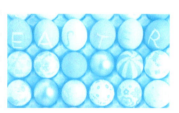

Many Christians begin the celebration with an Easter Vigil the night before, sometimes called Easter Eve or Holy Saturday. Other traditions include **the Easter egg hunt**— Easter egg hunts feature eggs hidden by the mythical Easter bunny, which may contain candy or other prizes. The children will go looking for eggs to put in their Easter egg baskets. On the day before Easter, many families decorate hard-boiled eggs with paint to use for the hunt.

Countries all over the world celebrate the holiday differently. Italy holds reenactments (重演) of the Easter story held in the public squares. Cyprus(塞浦路斯) holds bonfires in the yards of schools and churches. In Germany, eggs are set in trees, called Easter egg trees, similar to the Christmas tree.

Good Friday(耶稣受难日) is a Christian holiday commemorating the crucifixion of Jesus Christ and his death. It is observed on Friday before Easter Sunday.

Valentine's Day is a religious holiday too. It is an annual holiday celebrated on February 14, originated as a Western Christian feast day honoring one or more early saints named Valentinus. People buy cards, flowers, chocolates and other gifts for their beloved.

Boxing Day(节礼日), also called **St. Stephen's Day**, is a holiday celebrated the day after Christmas Day. It originated in England in the middle of the nineteenth century under Queen Victoria, and is now celebrated among the previous Commonwealth countries such as Britain, Ireland, Australia, Canada, etc. Traditionally, it was a custom for trades people, in Britain, to collect "Christmas boxes" of money or presents on the first weekday after Christmas as thanks for good service throughout the year. Nowadays, Boxing Day has lost its religious meaning and has become a shopping holiday, much like **Black Friday** in the USA (the day after Thanksgiving Day) and **Singles' Day** in China (also known as Double Eleventh Day). In the UK it is classed as a Bank Holiday.

2. British-specific Holidays

A bank holiday is a colloquial term for a public holiday in the United Kingdom, some Commonwealth countries, and the Republic of Ireland. Thus, the above-mentioned holidays such as Christmas Day, Easter Day, Good Friday, as well as New Year's Day are all part of bank holidays. In addition, the last Monday in May and August are respectively the Spring Bank Holiday and the Summer Bank Holiday in England and Wales. During bank holidays, banks close and the majority of the working population is granted time off work or extra pay for working on these days.

The Queen's Birthdays are specific to the UK. The Queen celebrates two birthdays each year: the Queen's Actual Birthday falls on April 21 and the Queen's Official Birthday takes place on a sunny Saturday in June. The official birthday of the Sovereign is marked each year by a military parade and march-past, known as **Trooping the Colour**(皇家阅兵仪式). Trooping the Colour around Buckingham Palace in London has marked the official birthday of the British sovereign since 1748. Elizabeth Ⅱ stopped riding to Trooping the Colour in 1986 and since then she has travelled in a carriage. The royalty members will attend the parade to celebrate Queen's birthday. Members of the royal family will gather on the balcony of Buckingham Palace for an RAF fly-past following the Trooping the Colour ceremony. In the UK, the monarch's birthday is also the National Day.

Guy Fawkes' Day(盖伊·福克斯日) also known as Bonfire Night or Firework Night, is a national festival annually held on November 5. It marks the anniversary of the discovery of a plot to blow up the Houses of Parliament in London in 1605. The attack was planned by a group of Catholic conspirators, which included Guy Fawkes. The explosives would have been set off when King James Ⅰ of England (King James Ⅵ of Scotland) and many parliamentary members were in the building. The conspirators were later arrested, tortured and executed. Many people light bonfires and set off fireworks on this night and in some towns and cities, the municipality organizes a bonfire and professional firework display in a park. However, Guy Fawkes' Day is not a bank holiday.

The United Kingdom is composed of four parts: England, Scotland, Wales and Northern Ireland. The local customs and festivals observed may vary to a great deal. **St. George's Day** has been a major feast and national holiday in England on a par with Christmas from the early 15th century. In Northern Ireland and the Republic of Ireland, people celebrate **St. Patrick's Day**(圣帕特里克日) each year to commemorate St. Patrick. In Wales, **St. David's Day**(圣大卫日) has been regularly celebrated since the canonization(正式宣布为圣徒) of David in the 12th century. **Burns Night** is celebrated in Scotland to commemorate the life of the poet Robert Burns, and **St. Andrew's Day** is regarded as the National Day of Scotland.

Ⅴ. Exercises

Multiple Choices: *Choose the best answer from the four choices given.*

1. *Love Actually* is a romantic comedy set during a frantic month before _____ in London.
    A. Thanksgiving   B. Valentine's Day
    C. Christmas   D. Halloween

2. In the movie the protagonists are connected with each other. For example David and Karen are _____ while Mia and Natalie are _____.
    A. close friends; workmates   B. siblings; neighbours
    C. workmates; close friends   D. neighbours; sisters

3. The movie tells stories _____ weeks before the holiday and the epilogue happens _____ week(s) after the holiday.
    A. 4; 2   B. 3; 3   C. 5; 1   D. 6; 2

4. Which of the following couples does not have a happy ending in the movie?
    A. David and Natalie.   B. John and Judy.
    C. Sarah and Karl.   D. Harry and Karen.

5. The last scene of the movie is taken at _____ where joyful faces are everywhere.
    A. a wedding ceremony   B. an airport
    C. a public gathering   D. a school auditorium

6. David knocks on many wrong doors to find Natalie and he is forced to do the following except _____.
    A. to sing a carol

Unit Four　Holidays

  B. to send season's greetings

  C. to apologize for his poor cabinet

  D. to perform in front of the whole school

7. Which of the following festivals is not a religious one?

  A. Good Friday.　　　　　　　　B. Valentine's Day.

  C. Queen's Birthday Parade.　　　D. Boxing Day.

8. Which of the following holidays is a bank holiday in the UK?

  A. St. Stephen's Day.　　　　　　B. St. George's Day.

  C. St. David's Day.　　　　　　　D. St. Patrick's Day.

▸ **Blank-filling**: *Fill in the blanks with the missing information.*

1. Many British household actors co-star in *Love Actually*, such as _____, _____, _____, etc.

2. The bank holiday is virtually the public holiday in Britain, such as _____, _____, _____, etc.

3. It is said that there are more than one hundred holidays and festivals across the UK, and some of them are observed regionally. England, Welsh, Scotland and Northern Ireland all have their own national days, respectively _____, _____, _____, and _____.

4. Generally speaking, _____ is the most important festival in the Western world; for the Christians, perhaps _____ is the most important.

5. Every year, the earliest bank holiday in the UK is _____ and the last is _____.

6. Queen celebrates her birthday twice: the real one in _____ and the other official one in _____, which often brings Britain hundreds of thousands of tourists each year. The highlight of Queen's Birthday Parade is also called _____.

7. Besides the holidays talked in Section A, I also know several cultural festivals, such as _____, _____, _____.

▸ **Translate & Appreciate**: *Translate the classic lines from the movie into Chinese and share your understandings.*

　　Whenever I get gloomy with the state of the world, I think about the arrivals gate at Heathrow Airport. General opinion's starting to make out that we live in a world of hatred and greed. But I don't see that, seems to me that love is everywhere. Often it's not particularly dignified or newsworthy, but it's always there, fathers and sons, mothers and daughters, husbands and wives, boyfriends, girlfriends, old friends. When the plane hit the Twin Tower, as far as I know, none of the phone calls from people on board were messages of hate or revenge. They are all messages of love. If you look for it, I've got a sneaky feeling that love actually is all around.

_____
_____
_____
_____

▶ **Voice Your Opinion**: *Read the following reviews about Love Actually and voice your opinions on this movie after you finish watching it.*

⟨1⟩

By Roger Ebert from *Chicago Sun-Times*, Nov. 7, 2003

Love Actually is a belly-flop into the sea of romantic comedy. It contains about a dozen couples who are in love. That's an approximate figure because some of them fall out of love and others double up or change partners. There's also one hopeful soloist who believes that if he flies to Milwaukee and walks into a bar he'll find a friendly Wisconsin girl who thinks his British accent is so cute that she'll want to sleep with him. This turns out to be true.

The movie is written and directed by Richard Curtis, the same man who wrote three landmarks in recent romantic comedy: *Four Weddings and a Funeral*, *Notting Hill* and *Bridget Jones's Diary*. His screenplay for *Love Actually* is bursting enough material for the next three. The movie's only flaw is also a virtue: It's jammed with characters, stories, warmth and laughs, until at times Curtis seems to be working from a checklist of obligatory movie love situations and doesn't want to leave anything out. In 129 minutes, it feels a little like a gourmet meal that turns into a hot-dog eating contest.

Key points: _____
_____
_____
_____

⟨2⟩

By David Sterritt, Film Critic of *The Christian Science Monitor*

Love Actually is an offbeat Christmas package, starting with its R rating. There are a few moments when I thought "Sex Actually" would be a more accurate title.

There's nothing wrong with aiming a Christmas picture at older folks, of course, and grown-ups will certainly be enticed by the glittering cast.

A romantic comedy-drama has to make sense, though, and *Love Actually* doesn't,

Unit Four Holidays

actually.

Set mostly in London, the picture has several stories. One features Hugh Grant as the Prime Minister who's infatuated with his assistant. Another follows an aging pop singer (Bill Nighy) who's all too honest about the sappiness of his new Christmas song. Yet another centers on a mystery writer (Colin Firth) and a Portuguese maid (Lucia Moniz) who fall in love.

There's also the Prime Minister's sister (Emma Thompson) and her straying husband (Alan Rickman), an office worker (Laura Linney) with a psychotic brother, a single dad (Liam Neeson) with a precocious kid, a duo of porn stars, and other characters.

You may find *Love Actually* less far-fetched than I did if you can believe that a Prime Minister—with Hugh Grant's looks and charm—has nothing to do on Christmas Eve but pout around his office. Or that the pop singer could get away with spouting obscenities on TV and radio shows. Or ... the examples are endless.

Sometimes the movie seems bent on sabotaging itself. The most poignant subplot, about Ms. Linney's character, is left dangling with no resolution. The picture tries to earn points by breaking stereotypes, then reaffirms them a few reels later—the Prime Minister is smitten with a chubby woman, for instance, but this twist comes undone with a string of nasty "fat jokes".

Watching all these is like looking under the Christmas tree and finding everything you ever wanted (all those stars!) and everything you don't want (all that bathroom humor!) shoved into one carelessly wrapped package. Open at your own risk.

Key points: _____

_____

_____

_____

Love Actually is made up of several interweaving stories. Which one touches you most? Whose performance caters for your taste?

Your opinion: _____

_____

_____

_____

_____

Section B   Groundhog Day

> For them the working hours are never long enough. Each day is a holiday, and ordinary holidays, when they come, are grudges as enforced interruptions in an absorbing vocation.
>
> —Winston Churchill

Ⅰ. Warm-up Questions

1. What day or holiday is the most important to you? And why?
2. What holidays originated from the USA?
3. If you woke up and found today was the repetition of yesterday, what would you feel and do?

Ⅱ. Basics about the Movie

Genre: fantasy, comedy
Director: Harold Ramis
Starring: Bill Murray
            Andie MacDowell
            Chris Elliott
Release Year: 1993
Running Time: 101 minutes
Country: the United States

Ⅲ. Synopsis

Phil Connors is a witty and charming weatherman on TV, but in real life he is bitter, appallingly self-centered, and he treats his co-workers with contempt, especially his new producer Rita and cameraman Larry.

Before the Groundhog Day, Phil, Rita, and Larry are sent on an assignment that Phil especially loathes: the annual Groundhog Day festivities in Punxsutawney, PA. An inexplicable thing happens after an unexpected blizzard traps them in the town: Phil seems to live the same day one after another—he meets the same people and is greeted with the exactly same words. No matter what efforts he makes, tomorrow never arrives.

At first Phil takes advantage of the time loop. But the more Phil relives the same day, the more he's forced to look at other people's lives, and something unusual happens: he begins to care about others. He tells his plight to Rita, and helps the needy in the town…

Will his efforts be appreciated and his affection to Rita be accepted?

IV. Culture Links

1. American Federal Festivals

Strictly speaking, there are no "national holidays" in the United States because the Congress only has constitutional authority to create holidays for federal institutions. So far there are ten annual US federal holidays on the calendar. Most federal holidays are also observed as state holidays, namely, **New Year's Day**, **Martin Luther King Jr. Day**, **Washington's Day**, **Memorial Day**, **Independence Day**, **Labor Day**, **Columbus Day**, **Veterans Day**, **Thanksgiving Day** and **Christmas Day**.

Some of the federal festivals are native to America, such as Washington's Day and Martin Luther King Jr. Day, both of which commemorate the birth of two important men in American history, Father of America and the pioneer fighter in American Civil Rights Movement. Columbus Day is established in veneration of the Italian explorer Christopher Columbus. Memorial Day is a day of  remembering the men and women who died while serving, while Veterans Day celebrates the service of all US military veterans. Memorial Day is observed on the last Monday of May; Veterans Day falls on the 11th of November, coinciding with Remembrance Day(英联邦阵亡将士纪念日) celebrated in the UK.

Independence Day

Independence Day is regarded as the birthday of the United States as a free and independent nation, commemorating the adoption of *The Declaration of Independence* on

July 4, 1776. Most Americans simply call it the "Fourth of July", on which date it always falls.

As the National Day of the United States, Independence Day is commonly associated with outdoor activities such as barbecues, picnics, baseball games, patriotic parades and some political speeches and ceremonies.

Thanksgiving Day

Historically, Thanksgiving has traditionally been a celebration of the blessings of the year, including the harvest. In the United States, the modern Thanksgiving holiday tradition can be traced back to the early 1600s. The popular belief is that the pilgrims came to the New Land in "the May Flower" and they had difficulty in settling down in Plymouth during the severe winter and the Indians taught them how to grow crops. The pilgrims celebrated the autumn harvest with a feast of thanks to God as well as to the native Americans. That's how the first Thanksgiving came into being.

Today Thanksgiving Day is a time for communal thanksgiving, feeling gratitude, lavish feasts, usually on the fourth Thursday of November in the United States. Squash, corn and turkey still appear on today's Thanksgiving tables and pumpkin pie and Indian pudding are traditional Thanksgiving desserts. And what Americans call the "Holiday Season" generally begins with Thanksgiving and lasts until the early January.

In the USA, one of the biggest Thanksgiving celebrations is Macy's Thanksgiving Day Parade, a tradition sponsored by chain department store Macy from the year of 1924. The Parade usually lasts for 3 hours from 9 a.m. and the whole process is broadcast live by NBC (National Broadcasting Company, 美国全国广播公司). In addition to the well-known balloons and floats, the Parade also features live music and other performances.

Thanksgiving Day is also celebrated in Canada, and some of the Caribbean islands. Different from the United States, Thanksgiving is celebrated a month earlier, on the second Monday of October in Canada.

2. American Non-Federal Holidays

Besides 10 federal holidays, there are a variety of holidays in the United States due to its complexity of its population and regional differences. Among the top ten most commonly celebrated holidays, Mother's Day lists the third after Christmas and Thanksgiving, Father's

Day, Halloween and Valentine's Day list respectively No. 7 to No. 9. And the celebration of some interesting holidays is relatively restricted to a smaller region.

Mother's Day & Father's Day

In many parts of the world such as Ancient Greece and China, there are holidays dedicated to mothers. The modern Mother's Day began in the early 20th century in the United States.

The first Mother's Day was celebrated in 1908, when Anna Jarvis held a celebration in memory of her mother at a church in Grafton, West Virginia. Ann Jarvis was a peace activist and she began to work at making "Mother's Day" a widely recognized holiday since 1905; her dream came true when President Woodrow Wilson signed a proclamation designating Mother's Day, held on the second Sunday in May, as a national holiday to honor mothers in 1914.

Many people send cards or gifts to their mother or mother figure or make a special effort to visit her. Common Mother's Day gifts are flowers, chocolate, candy, clothing, jewelry and treats, such as a beauty treatment or trip to a spa. Many worshippers celebrate the day with carnations, coloured if the mother is living and white if she is dead. Some families also organize an outing for all of their members or hold a special meal at home or in a restaurant. In the days and weeks before Mother's Day, many schools help their pupils prepare a handmade card or small gift for their mothers.

The creation of Father's Day was inspired by the celebration of Mother's Day, with its first celebration appearing in 1910. It was not until 1972 that Father's Day was made an official holiday in the United States. In America, Father's Day normally falls on the third Sunday of June and people wear red roses for their living fathers and white roses for the deceased ones.

Halloween

Halloween is a holiday well-received by children and it is traditionally celebrated on October 31. It is widely believed that many Halloween traditions originated from Celtic harvest festivals. From the Celtic religion come the custom of masquerading and the symbols of Halloween: ghosts, skeletons, devils, witches, black cats and owls. The jack-o'-

lantern is also of Celtic origin. It was an Irish custom to hollow out turnips or potatoes and place lighted candles inside them to scare evil spirits away from the house. When this custom was brought to the United States, the native pumpkin is used instead. Holes are cut in the pumpkin to make the eyes, nose and mouth and jack-o'-lanterns are usually placed by the window.

Trick-or-treat is a customary celebration for children on Halloween and they love to dress up in ghosts. Typical Halloween pranks are soaping windows, writing on doors with crayons, overturning ash-cans and sticking pins into doorbells to keep them ringing.

Groundhog Day(土拨鼠日)

February 2 is the date that is known as Candlemas(圣烛节) in Europe and Groundhog Day in America. Groundhog Day is believed to be an evolution of Candlemas in the New Continent.

Candlemas is a Roman Catholic festival celebrating the purification of the Virgin Mary (圣母玛利亚) after she gave birth to Jesus. In the Middle Ages many lighted candles were carried into the church for the Mass, a special kind of religious ceremony in the Roman Catholic Church, thus Candlemas got its name.

It was believed by many country folks that on Feb. 2 hibernating animals left their dens to inspect the state of the sky. Strangely enough, on this day good weather indicated a prolonged winter while clouds and chills indicated an early spring. If hibernating animals such as bears, badgers and particularly hedgehogs saw their shadows on that day, hibernation should be prolonged for several weeks. When this tradition was spread to the New Continent in its early days, the North American groundhog took the place of the Old World hedgehog.

Modern customs of the holiday involve early morning celebrations to watch the groundhog emerging from its burrow. Lots of tourists come to a small town, Punxatawney, in the state of Pennsylvania to see its town pet, a groundhog named Phil, "Punxatawney Phil". And this traditional holiday has received widespread attention as a result of the 1993 film *Groundhog Day*.

Ⅴ. Exercises

▸ **True or False Statements**: *Read the following statements and decide whether they are true (T) or false (F).*

  _____1. Phil Connors is a weatherman, who is eager to report the Groundhog Day this year with the new producer Rita.

  _____2. Phil wakes up on Feb. 3, only to find that it is just a copy of Feb. 2 and he feels distressed at first.

Unit Four Holidays

_____3. Nobody believes that Phil is trapped in the time loop with an exception of his high school friend.

_____4. In the movie the Punxatawney Phil is announced to see its shadow, which means springtime is not far away.

_____5. In the United States there are ten federal holidays, including Valentine's Day and Veterans Day.

_____6. Both Mother's Day and Halloween are of American origin.

_____7. In America, Thanksgiving Day is traditionally celebrated on the last Thursday in November; the same is true of Canada.

_____8. The traditional flowers for mothers on Mother's Day and for fathers on Father's Day are respectively carnations and roses.

_____9. Columbus Day and Groundhog Day are both exclusively observed in the United States.

_____10. Veterans Day falls on the same day with Remembrance Day in the UK and the Singles' Day in China.

Short-answer Questions: *Give brief answers to the following questions.*

1. What are the holidays or festivals originating from Christianity?

   _____
   _____
   _____

2. What are the holidays related to soldiers? List three, please.

   _____
   _____
   _____

3. What is the origin of Thanksgiving Day?

   _____
   _____
   _____

4. Some holidays are both bank holidays in the UK and federal holidays in the US. What are they?

   _____
   _____
   _____
   _____

英美经典影视与文化教程
Anglo-American Classic Movies and Culture

▶ **Extracurricular Exploration**: *Explore the Internet. Find more about the following holidays, and complete the following table. Make an introduction of two holidays on the basis of the finished table.*

Holidays	Date of Celebration	Symbols	Celebrating Countries	Featured Celebrations
Easter				
Guy Fawkes' Day				
Halloween				
Independence Day				
Queen's Birthday				
Christmas				
St. Patrick's Day				
Thanksgiving Day				

 Ⅵ. Critical Thinking

1. Columbus Day honors the day when Spanish explorer, Christopher Columbus, first arrived in the Americas on Oct. 12, 1492. It is a federal holiday; however, many people refuse to celebrate it. Do you know the reason? What's your opinion on this issue?

2. Thanksgiving Day is seldom celebrated in the UK and some of British people even detest the existence of such an American holiday. Can you figure out the reason?

Unit Four   Holidays

Section C   Rise of the Guardians

I. Movie Information (Explore and Find)

Genre: _____
Chinese Title: _____
Director: _____
Dubbing Stars: _____
Running Time: 97 minutes
Release Year: _____
Country: _____

▸ Use the information you have found to fill in the blanks.

Rise of the Guardians is a _____ (year) _____ (country) _____ (genre), which is adapted from William Joyce's *The Guardians of Childhood* book series and *The Man in the Moon* short film by Joyce and Reel FX Creative Studios. The film is a production of director _____. *Rise of the Guardians* was nominated for the Golden Globe Award for Best Animated Feature Film.

II. Synopsis

Rise of the Guardians is a 3D fantasy movie telling the story of how four Immortal Guardians team up to protect the hopes, beliefs and imagination of children all over the world when an evil spirit launches an assault on the Earth.

Jack Frost, the spirit of Winter, is invisible, so school kids don't believe in the existence of him, which annoys him a lot. Nicholas St. North is warned by the Man in the Moon that Pitch Black is threatening the children of the world with his nightmares. Subsequently, the Easter Bunny, Santa Claus, the Tooth Fairy, and the Sandman are called to arms. Jack Frost has been chosen to be a new Guardian though he is unimpressed by this position. It is Nicholas St. North that convinces Jack Frost and enlists his help.

Jack learns that baby teeth contain childhood memories of the children who lost them after visiting Tooth's world. Jack saves the Baby Tooth from being kidnapping when Pitch raids Tooth's home. As a result, the children's teeth can't be collected, thus preventing Tooth from sharing Jack's memories and causing children to not believe in Tooth. In order to thwart Pitch's plan, the group decides to collect children's teeth. During their journey, a quarrel between North and Bunny awakens a boy, Jamie, who still believes in Tooth because he can see everybody except for Jack. Pitch's nightmares then attack, provoking Sandy as the Guardian of Dreams. Jack aids, but Sandy is killed by Pitch.

As Easter draws near, the dejected Guardians gather in Bunny's home. With the unexpected aid of Jamie's little sister, Sophie, they begin the process of painting eggs for Easter. After Jack takes Sophie home, he is lured to Pitch's lair by a voice. Pitch taunts him with his memories and fear of non-belief, distracting him long enough for Pitch to destroy the eggs, causing children to stop believing in Easter and Bunny. Losing his trust in the Guardians, Jack isolates himself in Antarctica, where Pitch tries to convince him to join his side. When Jack refuses, Pitch threatens to kill Baby Tooth unless Jack gives him his staff. He agrees, but Pitch breaks Jack's staff and throws him down a chasm. Unlocking his memories, Jack learns that he was a mortal teenager who fell into ice while saving his younger sister. Inspired, Jack fixes his staff and returns to the lair to rescue the kidnapped baby fairies.

Every child in the world except Jamie disbelieves, weakening the Guardians. Finding Jamie's belief wavering, Jack makes it snow in his room, renewing belief and causing Jack to be seen and heard for the first time. Jack and Jamie gather the boy's friends, whose renewed belief bolsters their fight against Pitch. Pitch threatens them, but their dreams prove stronger than his nightmares, resulting in Sandy's resurrection. Defeated and disbelieved in, Pitch tries to retreat, but his nightmares, sensing his fear, turn on him and trap him in his lair. Afterward, Jamie and his friends bid goodbye to the Guardians as Jack accepts his place as the Guardian of Fun.

Ⅲ. Culture Links

1. Tooth Fairy

The Tooth Fairy is a fantasy figure in the legend. Children in many English-speaking countries hide their lost teeth under their pillows and fully expect them to be found by a fairy. It is likely that the Tooth Fairy derives from the European, particularly German tradition of placing a lost tooth in a mouse or rat hole. The folk believed that when a new tooth grew in, it would possess the dental qualities of whatever creature found it, but not of the original tooth. So the rodents were their choice of creatures. Then this fair exchange principle was brought to America by German immigrants and it is on this new land that the somewhat fearful "tooth rat" is replaced by a more agreeable fairy.

2. Festivals and Their Symbols

The **Easter Bunny** is a folkloric figure and symbol of Easter, depicted as a rabbit bringing Easter eggs. In the legend, the creature carries colored eggs in his basket, candy, and sometimes also toys to the homes of good children. Sometimes, it is also called the Easter Rabbit or Easter Hare.

The hare or rabbit is connected with Easter maybe because of the animal's association with the moon. There are several points of ancient folklore proving their resemblances: the animal is nocturnal(夜间活动的); the female carries her young for one month; according to a most curious belief both the hare and the moon have the power of changing their sex, since the new moon is masculine and the waning moon is feminine.

The Easter Bunny also originated in pre-Christian fertility lore. The hare and the rabbit were the most fertile animals our forefathers knew, so they selected them as a symbol of abundant new life in the spring season.

Santa Claus or Father Christmas is a sure symbol of Christmas, who is believed to deliver presents to good children on the Eve of Christmas. Santa Claus is generally depicted as a joyous, white-bearded man, wearing a red coat, red trousers, a black leather belt and boots. He will come on a sledge, carrying a big bag of gifts. Santa Claus is children's favorite.

The first Europeans who arrived in the New World brought St. Nicholas and his stories with them. In the sixteenth century, reformers and counter-reformers took every step possible to curb the Saint Nicholas-related customs, but they could not succeed. The common people in Europe loved
the Saint so much that not only did his customs survive in the European subcontinent, but they were later carried overseas as well.

IV. Expansion

Compare the festivals in three countries and write them down in the table.

	the UK	the US	China
The National Day			
Most important holiday			
Biggest shopping day			
Love-themed day			
Days for soldiers			
All celebrated holiday			

V. Fun Time

Love Is All Around is a soundtrack of the 1994-year movie *Four Weddings and a Funeral* by a Scottish band Wet Wet Wet. In *Love Actually*, it is adapted into *Christmas Is All Around*. Now let's listen to this enchanting song.

Love Is All Around
——Wet Wet Wet
I feel it in my fingers, I feel it in my toes
Love is all around me and so the feeling grows
It's written on the wind, it's everywhere I go
So if you really love me, come on and let it show

Unit Four Holidays

You know I love you I always will
My mind's made up by the way that I feel
There's no beginning, there'll be no end
'Cause on my love you can depend

I see your face before me, as I lay on my bed
I kinda get to thinking of all the things we said
You gave a promise to me and I gave mine to you
I need someone beside me in everything I do
You know I love you I always will
My mind's made up by the way that I feel
There's no beginning, there'll be no end
'Cause on my love you can depend
It's written on the wind, it's everywhere I go
So if you really love me, come on and let it show
Come on and let it show
Come on and let it show
Come on and let it show
Come on and let it show
Come on and let it show
Come on and let it show

Unit Five

Education

Section A   Dead Poets Society
Section B   The History Boys
Section C   Accepted

Preface

Western educational systems share some common characteristics with ours; the discrepancies are even wider. Every year an increasing number of Chinese students go abroad for study and the most popular destinations include the United States, the United Kingdom, Australia, etc.

In this unit, we will get closer to the campus in the UK and in the USA to know more about the exotic schools, students and faculties. *Dead Poets Society* brings us a dedicated English teacher who tries to teach his students to suck the narrow out of poetry and life; *The History Boys* facilitates us to know how Britain students knock on the doors of the renowned Oxbridge; and *Accepted* mocks the conventional college in a humorous way.

Unit Goals

- To know how the educational systems work in the UK and the USA;
- To tell the differences between Sino-Western education;
- To learn how to apply for a foreign university.

Unit Five   Education

Section A   Dead Poets Society

> The poem is never a put-up job. It begins as a lump in the throat, a sense of wrong, a homesickness, a loneliness. It is never a thought to begin with. It is at its best when it is a tantalizing vagueness.
>
> — On Poetry by Robert Frost

 I. Warm-up Questions

1. What is American high school life like in your mind's eyes? Is American high school students' life easier or tougher than their Chinese counterparts?

2. Teachers usually have great influence on their students. Have you ever met such an impressive teacher who left a deep impression on you? What are your criteria for a good teacher?

3. What should the relationship between teacher and student be like, in your mind?

 II. Basics about the Movie

Genre: drama
Director: Peter Weir
Starring: Robin Williams
Running Time: 128 minutes
Release Year: 1989
Country: the United States

III. Synopsis

Dead Poets Society is a 1989 film, telling the story of a great teacher who inspires his students to look at poetry with a different perspective of authentic knowledge and feelings. The story was set in 1959 at the fictional elite conservative Vermont boarding school Welton Academy.

Painfully shy Todd Anderson has been sent to the school where his popular older brother was valedictorian(毕业致辞的学生). His room-mate, Neil Perry, although exceedingly bright and popular, is very much under the thumb of his overbearing father. The two, along with their other friends, meet Professor Keating, their new English  teacher John Keating. Mr. Keating inspires his students to look at poetry with a different perspective of authentic knowledge and feelings. He also tells them of the Dead Poets Society, and encourages them to go against the status quo. Each, in their own way, does this, and they are all changed for life.

IV. Culture Links

1. A Panoramic View of Modern American Education System

American education commonly falls into three categories: public education, private education and home education. About 87% of school-age children attend public schools, about 10% attend private schools and roughly 3% are home-schooled.

K-12 education American public education covers the education from kindergarten, primary schools (Grade 1—6), secondary education (Grade 7—8 or 7—9), and high education (Grade 9—12 or 10—12), hence it is abbreviated as K-12. Schooling is compulsory for all children in the United States, but the age range for which school attendance is required varies from state to state.

During the elementary stage, the courses provided include reading, arithmetic, language, arts, science, social studies, music, art, and physical education. Secondary education can be further divided into junior high school and senior high school and the core curriculum include more specialized—English, social studies, algebra, geometry, etc.

* * *

Public school vs. Private school K-12 students in most areas have a choice between free tax-funded public schools and privately funded schools. Public school systems are supported by a combination of local, state, and federal government funding while private schools usually generate their own funding from a variety of sources such as tuition, private grants, and fundraising from parents, alumni, and other community members. Besides, if the private school is associated with a religious group, the local branch may provide an important source of funding as well.

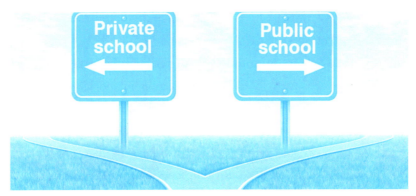

The most obvious discrepancy between public and private schools comes down to tuitions. Public schools cannot charge tuition but on the other hand, public schools are complicated, often underfunded operations influenced by political winds and shortfalls. Private schools charge varying rates depending on geographic location, the school's expenses, and the availability of funding from sources, other than tuition. Average day-schools charge normally from around $10,000 to $17,000, boarding schools double. The benefit of private schools lies in its independence: they do not have to follow the same sorts of regulations and bureaucratic processes that govern (and sometimes hinder) public schools; they are highly specialized, offering differentiated learning, advanced curriculum, or programs geared toward specific religious beliefs.

The admission procedures are also different. By law, public schools must accept all children. Private schools are selective in admitting new students. They are not obligated to accept every child, so getting admitted may involve in-depth applications with multiple interviews, essays, and testing. Other discrepancies in teachers, class size, and curriculum also exist.

After obtaining the high school diploma, the high school grad can either choose to learn a trade, find employment or apply for a college to pursue their education. According to the statistics released by the US Bureau of Labor, in October 2016, about seventy percent of 2016 high school graduates were enrolled in colleges or universities.

2. SAT & ACT

In the USA, there is no such big day as the College Entrance Examination in China. College applicants are chosen according to the following four aspects: high school records usually measured by GPA (grade point average, 绩点), high school teacher's recommendations, the impression they make during the interviews in the university and the score of SAT or ACT.

SAT, short form of **Scholastic Aptitude Test** or **Scholastic Assessment Test**, is one of the standardized tests widely used for college application in the USA. Its history can be dated back as far as 1926. Every year SAT will be held on the first Saturday of March, May, June, October, November and December and the last Saturday of January. The March SAT test is only held in America. After the reform in 2016, SAT is composed of four sections totaling 1,600 grades: Reading, Writing and Language, Math (no calculator), and Math (calculator allowed). Besides, the test taker may optionally write an essay for another 50 minutes.

ACT, or **American College Testing**, is the other leading US college admissions test measuring what high school graduates learn in high school to determine their academic readiness for college. It was first administrated in 1959.

At present every year ACT is held 6 times, respectively in February, April, June, September, October and December. The February test is limited in America. ACT contains 215 multiple-choice tests in four areas: English, mathematics, reading and science and the test lasts 175 minutes. ACT's writing test is optional and will not affect the tester's composite score. The full mark for ACT is 36. All four-year colleges and universities in the USA accept ACT, but different institutions place different emphases on standardized tests.

3. Higher Education

The history of American higher education is not long but in the past century America has established a handful of world-famous colleges or higher-education institutions. Colleges are also labeled as public ones and private ones.

The Ivy League commonly refers to the eight prestigious private institutions of higher education in the Northeastern United States, including Harvard University, Brown University, Columbia University, Princeton University, Dartmouth College, Cornell University, Yale University and the University of Pennsylvania.

Ivy League schools are generally viewed as some of the most prestigious, and are ranked among the best universities worldwide. According to US *News & World Report* 2017, Harvard, Princeton and Columbia rank among the best top ten universities worldwide with Harvard topping the ranking.

Many social elite graduated from the Ivy League, so did the American presidents. Of the forty-four men who have served as President of the United States, fifteen have graduated from Ivy League universities. Of them, eight have degrees from Harvard, five from Yale, three from Columbia, two from Princeton and one from Pennsylvania. The latest five US presidents all graduated from the Ivy League: George H. W. Bush, Bill Clinton and George W. Bush from Yale, Barack Obama from both Columbia and Harvard, and Donald Trump from Pennsylvania.

Aside from the Ivy League, America has many other top-ranking universities such as MIT (Massachusetts Institute of Technology), Stanford University, University of California, Berkeley, etc.

V. Exercises

▶ **Multiple Choices**: *Choose the best answer from the four choices given.*
  1. Which is true about the film *Dead Poets Society*?
     A. It is a British film telling the story in a private high school.
     B. Welton Academy is a prestigious school that prepares students, both male and female, for college.
     C. Dead Poets Society was originally a school literary club.
     D. Robin Williams starred and directed the film, which brought him the honor of Best Actor in 1990's Oscar.

2. Why does Mr. Keating ask students to tear off pages?

   A. Because personally he dislikes those pages.

   B. Because he wants his students to think independently.

   C. Because he wants to shock his students.

   D. Because those pages are misprinted.

3. How do people react to the Keating's way of teaching?

   A. Mr. McAllister frowns upon his method at first.

   B. Students think he has temporarily gone mad.

   C. All students do as he tells without any hesitation.

   D. No one follows his advice.

4. What is Dead Poets Society?

   A. A social club for boys and girls who love poetry.

   B. A group of poetry-lovers who search for the essence of life.

   C. A study group of poetry-lovers to get good grades.

   D. A school club to study poets who have passed away long ago.

5. Which is closest in meaning to "Carpe Diem"?

   A. Study hard.   B. Never lose hope.

   C. Hold fast to dreams.   D. Seize the day.

6. Which college is not a member of the Ivy League?

   A. Yale.   B. Princeton.

   C. Stanford.   D. Harvard.

7. What's NOT true about the American education?

   A. The majority of students choose to attend the public school.

   B. Students have the freedom of choosing public education, private education or even home education.

   C. Private schools are superior to public schools in every way.

   D. Most top universities in the US are private ones.

8. Which of the following statements about SAT and ACT is true?

   A. High school graduates can choose which exam to sit in for.

   B. Both SAT and ACT are held seven times a year.

   C. The history of SAT is earlier than that of ACT, so it is more popular.

   D. ACT is more useful in applying for famous universities.

Unit Five Education

▶ **Blank-filling**: *Fill in the blanks with the missing information.*

1. The four pillars of Welton Academy are _____, _____, _____, _____.

2. In the film, Mr. Keating asks students to call him "Captain", which comes from the poem _____ written by American poet _____. This poem is to venerate the former president _____. The other poem mentioned in this film is _____, which is the masterpiece of American poet _____.

3. Mr. Keating thinks _____ and _____ are both major themes in poetry; in reading poetry, he encourages his students to strive to _____ instead of just considering what the author thinks.

4. There are usually four steps for a high school graduate to apply for a college in the United States: _____, _____, _____, and _____.

5. Both _____ and _____ are exams the high school graduates normally will take, and writing is optional in either exam. The full marks of the two exams, presently, are respectively _____ and _____.

▶ **Translate & Appreciate**: *Translate the classic lines from the movie into Chinese and share your understandings.*

1. Oh, I live to be the ruler of life, not a slave.

   _____
   _____
   _____

2. Learn to think for yourselves again. No matter what anybody tells you, words and ideas can change the world.

   _____
   _____
   _____

3. Because, you see, gentlemen, these boys are now fertilizing daffodils. But if you listen real close… you can hear them whisper their legacy to you. Seize the day, boys. Make your lives extraordinary.

   _____
   _____
   _____
   _____

4. We don't read and (or, 编者注) write poetry because it's cute. We read and write poetry because we are members of the human race. And the human race is filled with passion. And medicine, law, business, engineering—these are noble pursuits and necessary to sustain life. But poetry, beauty, romance, love—these are what we stay alive for.

___

___

___

___

▶ **Voice Your Opinion**: *Read the following two reviews about Dead Poets Society and voice your opinions on this movie after you finish watching it.*

〈1〉

Carpe Diem, Because the Days don't Stand Still

By netizen blissfulmitch, 4 February 2005

First of all, this movie is my all-time favorite, out of all the hundreds of films I have seen. However, every time I mention this film, I have to answer most people's quizzical looks with "It's a beautiful little 80s film that stayed in the 80s." After seeing it for the 24th time since I first saw it 5 years ago, on my 13th birthday, I can gladly say that this movie went far and beyond the 80s, and the power and inspiration of the message can be felt every day.

Dead Poets Society is a most underrated film by a most underrated director whose inspiring, uplifting and moral tales firmly grounded in reality are not nearly as appreciated as they should be. Here, we see one of his very personal and cradled projects, and he shows the visual style and concentration on characters in which he is so affluent. His control of the camera and the characters are very strong and very smooth. The cinematography is near perfect, with every shot, along with the editing, seamless. Also very compelling are the color-tones in every scene, perfectly matching the mood and events of the scene. Could you say this is art? Absolutely.

Then we have the performances. Robin Williams continues in stride as one who has to-date remained the most touching, heart-wrenching, awe-inspiring comedian with inarguable acting talent (he still remains my most favorite performer on the film screen). His Professor John Keating is a man who embodies every professor who you thought was cool and respectable, every person who taught or enlightened you in something out of the ordinary. In fact—dare I say it?—he teaches something EXTRAORDINARY! We have the tragically underrated Robert Sean Leonard in his role as the free-thinking catalyst student Neil. Why is this man not a household name/Hollywood heavyweight? His roles are always full of inspiration, energy, and tragic emotion that never fail to move the audience. His role in this movie is fresh, unhindered, and never pretentious as the cautionary tale of the movie. And then we have Ethan Hawke in one of his earliest roles as the point-of-view character. The entire supporting cast is very strong, also, providing the foundation and serves as the various emotional ties that further involve us in the story. Josh Charles's role as Knox Overstreet is a role that almost all guys can relate to wholeheartedly. And of course, all the actors who are in *Dead Poets Society* do a fine job.

And lastly, the story. I won't summarize it since it's been summarized many times here, but I will say that it is one of the best coming of age stories for not only adolescents, but anyone. I have personally heard from nine-to-fivers who were inspired by this movie to change the situations of their jobs, careers, relationships for the better. I first saw this movie when I was 13, and immediately stamped, crowned and elevated this movie as my all-time favorite. Now that I am 18 and living on my own, with very different concerns than back then, I turn back to this movie over and over again, to find inspiration, solace and of course, entertainment. It is still my all-time favorite, and it still inspires me to seize the day and make my life extraordinary.

Key points: _____
_____
_____
_____

A Powerful Antidote to Conformism

By Francisco Huerta, 22 August 2001

There are certain films that get under your skin, never to come out. They change your life, subtly altering your perceptions of reality, almost always for the better.

Dead Poets Society is one of those few films.

I saw the movie back when I was in high school. I had a teacher who told us that we really needed to watch it; in fact, it was our "homework" for the day. We didn't need to bring back a report, or talk about it in class. All he asked from us was to watch it, make up our own mind about it, and that was it. As you can imagine, many friends of mine didn't watch it at all; I did. And yes, I feel I changed a bit from then on.

Back when you are young, you never really stop to think what in the world you are doing with your life. You simply live for the day, hope your grades will be enough to pass, and that's it. Long term thinking involves maybe flirting with a girl. Nothing more. What this film showed me was that we have the responsibility and the joy of being alive on this planet. That we are dust, and we will go back to it, so we have precious little time to make a difference. That we have a moral obligation to "seize the day, and make our lives extraordinary" (my favorite quote in all movie history). That the world, basically is ours. That the only limitations are within ourselves, and that we owe it to us to fight, to rebel against conformity, to change what we hate and keep what we love. That living in this world is a beautiful responsibility, and that only cowards dare not change it for the better.

The fact that the cast was basically my age, and was passing through the same dilemmas and situations I was facing made it all so much more powerful.

So here I sit, 12 years from that day. I still don't think I have seized the day completely. But I keep on trying; I always will. I wonder how many people were transformed by this gem of a movie; I hope many.

10 out of 10. A definitive masterpiece.

Key points: _____

_____

_____

_____

Mr. Keating, undoubtedly, is a man of knowledge and wisdom. He refuses to be stuck in a rut and accordingly, does not teach in the conventional way. Instead, he encourages his students to follow their hearts and inspires them to learn and to think with their head. How do you like such a teacher? Do you think a teacher like Keating will be well received in Chinese senior high schools? Have you ever met a teacher whose instructions still linger on your mind?

Your opinion: _____

_____

_____

_____

 Ⅵ. Poetry Appreciation

The Road Not Taken is a poem by American poet Robert Frost, published in 1916 as the first poem in the collection *Mountain Interval*. It is the poet's most well-known and also controversial poem. Read the poem and share your interpretation with your teacher and classmates.

The Road Not Taken

Robert Frost

Two roads diverged in a yellow wood,
And sorry I could not travel both
And be one traveler, long I stood
And looked down one as far as I could
To where it bent in the undergrowth;

Then took the other, as just as fair,
And having perhaps the better claim,
Because it was grassy and wanted wear;
Though as for that the passing there
Had worn them really about the same,
And both that morning equally lay

In leaves no step had trodden black.
Oh, I kept the first for another day!
Yet knowing how way leads on to way,
I doubted if I should ever come back.

I shall be telling this with a sigh
Somewhere ages and ages hence:
Two roads diverged in a wood, and I—
I took the one less traveled by,
And that has made all the difference.

英美经典影视与文化教程
Anglo-American Classic Movies and Culture

Section B The History Boys

> School life is reminiscent of wild pranks, homework, and detention. However, an important aspect of school life was our relationship with teachers. We have had our share of lovable and irritating teachers.
>
> —Marcus Tullius Cicero

I. Warm-up Questions

1. Do you know what grammar school is? How about eleven-plus examination?
2. What is Oxbridge? What is the Russell Group?
3. How do you sum up your high school life? Are there any impressive teachers or classmates?

II. Basics about the Movie

Genre: comedy, drama
Director: Nicholas Hytner
Starring: Richard Griffiths,
　　　　　Clive Merrison Frances de la Tour
　　　　　Stephen Campbell Moore
Running Time: 109 minutes
Release Year: 2006
Country: the United Kingdom

III. The Synopsis

The movie is adapted from the British playwright Alan Bennett's play of the same title. It relates the story of an unruly(任性,不守规矩的) class of gifted and charming teenage boys taught by two eccentric and innovative teachers in the 1980s in Britain.

In a boys' grammar school in Sheffield in 1983, eight bright students—Crowther, Posner, Dakin, Timms, Akthar, Lockwood, Scripps, and Rudge—achieve high in the A-level and they are prepared to win a place at Oxford or Cambridge.

Bounced between their maverick(标新立异的) English teacher Hector, a young and shrewd professor Irwin hired to raise up their test scores, a grossly outnumbered history teacher Mrs Dorothy Lintott, and a headmaster Felix obsessed with results, the boys attempt to sift through it all to pass the daunting university admissions process. Their journey becomes as much about how education works, as it is about where education leads.

Ⅳ. Culture Links

1. A Panoramic View of Modern Britain Education System

As in the USA, there are two parallel school systems in Britain for primary and secondary education: the state system and the independent system. Between the ages of 5 to 11, the majority of students attend the free state schools. They are called co-educational or mixed schools because they admit both boys and girls.

When it comes to the secondary education, there are normally three choices: comprehensive schools which admit all the students; grammar schools accept students on the basis of their academic achievement or aptitude, usually in the form of 11-plus examinations; and secondary modern school.

There are about 2,500 independent schools in Britain and most of them are boy schools or girl schools, including well-renowned Eton, Winchester, and Roedean.

Britain's universities are legally independent and enjoy complete academic freedom. Admission is by selection based on A-level results, school references and an interview.

In England and Wales, the school year generally runs from early September until late July of the following year. Most schools operate a three-term school year, each term divided in half by a week-long break known as "half term". The three terms are autumn, spring and summer terms. Another point worth mentioning is that in the UK it usually takes students three years to obtain a bachelor's degree, one more year for a master's degree, and three to four years for a doctoral degree.

* * *

The Russell Group is a self-selected association presently of 24 public research universities in the United Kingdom. The group is widely perceived as representing the best universities in the UK. The Russell Group was formed in 1994 and the initial 17 member research universities were Birmingham, Bristol, Cambridge, Edinburgh, Glasgow, Imperial College London, Leeds, Liverpool, London School of Economics, Manchester, Newcastle, Nottingham, Oxford, Sheffield, Southampton, University College London and Warwick. Seven more universities joined the group subsequently: Cardiff University and King's College London in 1998, Queen's University Belfast in 2006, and four more universities in 2012: Exeter, Durham, Queen Mary University of London and York.

* * *

Oxbridge refers to two world-prestigious universities in Britain: Oxford and Cambridge. These two universities both have a long history and they compete with each other as they rival each other in prestige. Stephen Hawking is one of the few who attended them both.

As the oldest university in the English-speaking world, Oxford is a unique and historic institution. There is no clear date of foundation, but teaching existed at Oxford in some form in 1096 and developed rapidly from 1167, when Henry Ⅱ banned English students from attending the University of Paris. The 850-year-old Oxford has 11 kings, 6 Britain kings, 47 Nobel Prize winners, more than 50 presidents or prime ministers, such as Bill Clinton, David Cameron, Tony Blair, Margaret Thatcher, actors Rowan Atkinson, Hugh Grant, and Qian Zhongshu(钱钟书).

Cambridge was founded in 1209 by some scholars who left Oxford. It has 31 colleges and consists of over 100 departments, research centers, plus a central administration. Cambridge has more Nobel Prize winners than any other institution in the world. So far 90 Nobel Prize winners once worked at or graduated from Cambridge. The outstanding Chinese alumni include Xu Zhimo(徐志摩) and Louis Cha(查良镛).

▶ 2. A-levels

A-levels, a short form of General Certificate of Education Advanced Level, are a selection of advanced courses taken by students in the United Kingdom as a prerequisite for college or direct access to a career. A-levels are a full-time, two-year program that is made up of two components, Advanced Subsidiary (AS) and A2, although it is also possible to take A-levels on a part-time basis. The majority of students enroll onto an A-level course at the ages of 16~19 as a prequel to application to a university.

There are hundreds of A-Level subjects for the students to choose from and normally they will choose 3~4 subjects that really interest them. A-Levels will be held twice a year usually in May or June and October or November, and are graded A ~ E with outcomes being posted in August and March.

3. Grammar School(文法学校)

A **grammar school** is one of several different types of school in the history of education in the United Kingdom and other English-speaking countries, originally a school teaching Latin, but more recently an academically-oriented secondary school, differentiated in recent years from less academic secondary modern schools.

Today, "grammar school" commonly refers to one of the 164 remaining fully selective state-funded schools in England and the 69 remaining in Northern Ireland. Then how to win a place in the grammar school? The answer is to take an eleven-plus exam. The **eleven-plus** (11-plus) is an examination administered to some students in England and Northern Ireland in their last year of primary education, which governs admission to grammar schools and other secondary schools which use academic selection.

The examination tests a student's ability to solve problems using a test of verbal reasoning and non-verbal reasoning, with most tests now also offering papers in mathematics and English. The intention was that the eleven-plus should be a general test for intelligence similar to an IQ test, but with the addition of testing for taught curriculum skills the test now measures aptitude for school work.

V. Exercises

True or False Statements: *Read the following statements and decide whether they are true (T) or false (F).*

_____1. *The History Boys* is originally a play-adapted film.

_____2. The film tells the stories happening between four teachers and eight students in a boys' grammar school.

_____3. Tom Irwin graduates from the Corpus College of Oxford and he is invited to give the boys a push in applying for Oxbridge.

_____4. All the boys finally make their way into Oxbridge except poor Rudge.

_____5. Hector is fired due to his inappropriate actions and he is later killed on his way home in an accident.

_____ 6. Posner wins a scholarship and he finally chooses to be a teacher, teaching in Hector's way.

_____ 7. Unlike China, there are usually three terms (spring, autumn, winter) each academic year in the UK.

_____ 8. Oxford has a longer history than Cambridge while the latter has more Nobel Prize winners than the former.

_____ 9. Only those who perform well in the eleven-plus exam have the possibility of being admitted into grammar schools.

_____ 10. Education in Britain is compulsory for all children between the ages of 6 and 15.

▶ **Short-answer Questions**: *Give brief answers to the following questions.*

1. What is Oxbridge?

   _____

2. What are the three common types of secondary schools in Britain?

   _____

3. Name five of members of the Russell Group.

   _____

4. How is the A-level result graded?

   _____

5. When applying for a college position in Britain, what steps should a student take?

   _____

▶ **Extracurricular Exploration**: *Explore the Internet. Find out the answers to the following questions and make a no-more-than-5-minute presentation.*

1. In the UK in the primary and secondary educational stages, the number of boys' schools and girls' schools surpasses that of the mixed schools. Can you explain this phenomenon and voice your stand?

2. How do you like the three teachers in the movie, Hector, Dorothy, and Irwin? Justify your choice.

Unit Five   Education

Section C   Accepted

I. Movie Information (Explore and Find)

Genre: comedy
Chinese Title: _____
Director: _____
Starring: _____
Running Time: _____ minutes
Release Year: 2006
Country: _____

► Use the information you have found to fill in the blanks.

The movie *Accepted* is a 2006 comedy directed by _____, starring _____. The movie tells the story of a group of high school grads (Bartleby) who fail in applying for a college for one reason or another except _____, who succeeds in entering an imaginary college _____ as the family wishes.

In order not to disappoint his parents, Bartleby asks for the help from his best friend Sherman Schrader Ⅲ to create a virtual college _____ (SHIT). What happens next is totally out of his expectations. *Accepted* receives mixed reviews from audiences and critics.

II. Synopsis

Bartleby Gaines is a senior from a high school in Ohio. He fails to receive any acceptance letter from all of the colleges for which he applies. His best friend Sherman Schrader Ⅲ, on the other hand, has been accepted into his father's prestigious alma mater, Harmon College. Several of his friends are also rejected either due to legacy preferences, injury or personal intelligence.

In an attempt to gain approval from his strict father, Bartleby creates a fake college, the South Harmon Institute of Technology (SHIT), with the help of his friends. To make the invented college seem legitimate, Bartleby convinces Sherman to create a functional website for the school, which makes the matter even worse later.

To make the lie seem true, they lease an abandoned psychiatric hospital next to Harmon College and renovate it to look like a real one with the tuitions from parents; they even hire Sherman's peculiar uncle, a former professor from Harmon College. A group of rejected students gather around SHIT after being accepted by clicking on its website. Those young outcasts create their own curricula and they learn their dream majors, ranging from the culinary arts, sculpting, meditations, to unusual courses such as psycho kinesis(精神力). They enjoy their life and study in SHIT; meanwhile, Schrader is abused by his brothers in the BKE of Harmon College.

Clashes begin when the adjacent college is to build a new gateway. Bartleby refuses to relinquish the lease. SHIT is on the verge of closedown, and Bartleby makes an impassioned speech on the educational accreditation hearing…

Ⅲ. Culture Links

1. Fraternity and Sorority

Fraternities(兄弟会) and sororities(姐妹会) are generally referred to as Greek Life because they usually have three-Greek-word names. Fraternities are for male and sororities are for female, but now some fraternities admit them both. The members call each other brother or sister.

Fraternities have a long history in American colleges and universities. The oldest active social American college fraternity is Kappa Alpha Society founded in 1825 at Union College. Sigma Phi Society (1827) and Delta Phi Fraternity (1827) were founded in the same school and comprise the Union Triad.

Fraternities can be organized for many purposes, including university education, work skills, ethics, ethnicity, religion, politics, etc. On college campuses, fraternities may be divided into four different groups: social, service, professional and honorary. It is generally accepted that an explicit goal of fraternities is mutual support.

Fraternities are mentioned in many a movie such as *Legally Blond*, *Old School*, and *Animal House*, etc. In the movie fraternities are often depicted as a secret club, usually of the social type, and the members attend parties, drink alcohol, and even take drugs; BKE in the *Accepted* is such a social fraternity. Many celebrities in the US joined fraternities in college, for example, ex-President Gorge Bush was a member of Skull and Bones in Yale and President Donald Trump of Phi Gamma Delta.

2. College Application

The college admission process can be intimidating, but is also an exciting opportunity to showcase your talents, achievements, and perspective. Specific details vary by country and institution.

Most colleges and universities in the US have their own set of requirements for the information that is necessary for a college application. First of all, a common requirement on a college application is the applicant's standardized test score, most commonly ACT or SAT, and a high school transcript. Next, some colleges also require applications to include a letter of recommendation from the teacher and a personal essay as well. A commonly accepted application used by many universities is the "Common Application" which is an online application that is used by over 500 colleges and universities. Deadlines for admission applications are established and published by each college or university.

Almost all British universities are members of UCAS (Universities and Colleges Admissions Service), a clearing house for undergraduate admissions. Applicants submit a single application for up to 5 courses at different universities. There is a maximum limit of 4 choices for medicine, dentistry and veterinary science courses.

The application also includes current and expected qualifications, employment, criminal history, a personal statement, and a reference (which generally includes predicted grades if the applicant is still in education).

Additional forms are required for application to Oxbridge. One can only apply for a particular college at Oxford or Cambridge in a single year. Many Oxbridge applicants are assessed through academic interviews and sometimes further testing.

Anglo-American Classic Movies and Culture

 IV. **Expansion**

Find top private schools both in the UK and USA to have a comparison.

	the UK		the USA	
	Eton	St. Paul's Girls' School	George Stevens Academy	The Grier School
History				
Tradition				
Creed				
Alumni				
Features				

 V. **Fun Time**

Sports and other extracurricular activities are very popular in schools. Let's watch the video clip from the movie *High School Musical* to find more.

Unit Six

British Royalty

Section A　The Queen
Section B　The King's Speech
Section C　Henry VIII

Preface

The modern Great Britain is a country of constitutional monarchy, a system in which the monarch acts as a non-party political head of state under the constitution, whether written or unwritten.

Today, the role of the British monarch is by convention effectively ceremonial; with few exceptions, the monarch is bound by constitutional convention to act on the advice of the government. Let's get closer to several British monarchs and gain an insight into the mysterious British Royalty.

Unit Goals

- To have a deep understanding of the coming of the constitutional monarchy system;
- To understand the responsibilities and privileges of being a monarch;
- To have a general idea of the outstanding monarchs in British history.

Anglo-American Classic Movies and Culture

Section A　The Queen

> I declare before you all that my whole life, whether it be long or short, shall be devoted to your service and the service of our great imperial family to which we all belong.
>
> —Elizabeth II

I. Warm-up Questions

1. How many countries still have the royal family in the modern world? What are they?
2. *The Queen* relates the story about the world's oldest reigning monarch as well as Britain's longest-lived queen. Do you know who she is?
3. How many queens are there in the history of the UK?

II. Basics about the Movie

Genre: biography, drama, history
Director: Stephen Frears
Starring: Helen Mirren
　　　　　Michael Sheen
Running Time: 103 minutes
Release Year: 2006
Country: the United Kingdom

III. Synopsis

The movie revolves around what happened in the year 1997 and a sequence of events the Queen must face up to: The 44-year-old Tony Blair wins the election and becomes the youngest Prime Minister in history. The Queen—Elizabeth II is wary of Blair and his pledge to modernize Britain. Three months later, the ex-royal family member Diana Spenser, who divorced Prince Charles the year before, was killed in a car crash in Paris.

Opinions differ as to the scale of the funeral. The Royal families incline to hold a private funeral instead of an official Royal one while the government and Charles frown on it. Tony Blair delivers a speech in which he calls Diana "the People's Princess" and a flood of British people begin to gather before the Buckingham Palace to express their mourning towards the deceased. The heart-broken publics request the Queen to comfort her people.

During the following days the Royal family's popularity plummets, worsened by the reports from the media. Consequently, Blair recommends three strong measures to regain public confidence of the monarch: attend a public funeral for Diana at Westminster Abbey, fly a Union flag at half-mast over Buckingham Palace, and speak to the nation about Diana's life and legacy in a televised address.

After much hesitation and rejection from her husband and mother, the Queen finally decides to follow Blair's advice, returns to London to visit the mass outside the Buckingham Palace, and makes a public statement on live television, acknowledging Diana to be an unexceptional and talented human being. Two months later, the popularity of the monarch regains and the crisis is over.

Ⅳ. Culture Links

1. Queens in the UK

There are altogether six queens in British history, namely Mary Ⅰ, Elizabeth Ⅰ, Mary Ⅱ, Queen Anne, Queen Victoria and Elizabeth Ⅱ.

Mary Ⅰ and Elizabeth Ⅰ were half-sisters, with King Henry Ⅷ being their father. Mary Ⅰ was the only daughter of Henry Ⅷ and his first wife Catherine of Aragon to survive to adulthood. She became the first queen regnant of England from 1553 to 1558 after the death of her half-brother Edward Ⅵ. Mary Ⅰ was described as courageous and stubborn. Her character was moulded by her early years. Her executions of Protestants led to the posthumous sobriquet "**Bloody Mary**".

Elizabeth Ⅰ, the last Tudor monarch, was the daughter of Henry Ⅷ and his second wife, Anne Boleyn. Elizabeth Ⅰ, also called **Queen of Virgin**, was one of the greatest dictators in British history. Her 45-year reign (1558—1603) is generally considered one of the most glorious in British history. During her reign, England advanced in such areas as foreign trade, exploration, literature and the arts, and the age of exploration began: claiming new lands for England and introducing new materials and foods.

Mary Ⅱ and Queen Anne were sisters, both the daughters of James Ⅱ. Mary Ⅱ ruled England with her husband William from 1689 to 1694. William and Mary, both Protestants, became King and Queen regnant following the **Glorious Revolution**, which resulted in the adoption of *The Bill of Rights* and the deposition of her Roman Catholic father, James Ⅱ. William and Mary had no children.

Queen Anne became Britain's fourth queen in 1702 after the death of her brother-in-law William. Anne was plagued by ill health throughout her life. Anne was married to George of Denmark; though it was an arranged marriage, they were faithful and devoted partners.

Queen Victoria was the great-great-grandmother of Elizabeth Ⅱ, the current ruling queen of the UK. During her reign (1837—1901), Great Britain was a "constitutional monarchy" and thus the sovereign held relatively little direct political power. Her reign of 63 years and seven months is known as the **Victorian era**. It was a period of industrial, cultural, political, scientific, and military change within the United Kingdom, and was marked by a great expansion of the British Empire.

Elizabeth Alexandra Mary, also known as Elizabeth Ⅱ, is the elder daughter of King George Ⅵ. The coronation (加冕礼) of Queen Elizabeth Ⅱ as monarch of the United Kingdom, Canada, Australia, New Zealand, South Africa, Pakistan and Ceylon took place on 2 June 1953 at Westminster Abbey. She married Philip, Duke of Edinburgh at Westminster Abbey and their marriage has lasted more than 70 years. They have four children, three princes—Charles, Andrew, Edward and one princess Anne.

On 10 September, 2015, she broke the record of Queen Victoria and became the longest ruling monarch in British history. In October 2016, she became the longest

currently reigning monarch and head of state.

2. British Monarchy

The British monarchy is one of the oldest established monarchies in the world, and although it has changed quite a bit in the intervening centuries, the British monarch is still one of the most recognizable world figures.

"*The Queen reigns, but she does not rule.*" As the current monarch, Queen Elizabeth II is Head of the State, Head of the Armed Forces, and Head of the England Church. As a result, Queen Elizabeth appoints ministers, judges, diplomats, bishops, governors and some officers in the armed forces. She is head of the executive branch of government in Great Britain and must officially assent to a Bill from Parliament in order to make it become a law. Under the British constitution, executive authority lies with the monarch; however, in current practice, this authority is exercised only by, or on the advice of, the Prime Minister and the Cabinet.

The Queen does enjoy some privileges: she's completely immune from prosecution; she doesn't have to pay tax for her salary and income though she voluntarily began paying her fair share in 1992; she is the only person in the UK who doesn't legally need a license number or a number plate; she celebrates two birthdays each year, one in April and the official one in June.

The Queen also bears responsibilities and she has to carry out government duties, too. Every day piles of documents are delivered to the desk of the Queen waiting to be read or signed if necessary. The Queen represents the nation at times of great celebration or sorrow, such as the opening ceremony of 2012 London Olympic Games, **Remembrance Day** ceremony each year in Whitehall. Queen's Christmas message is broadcast annually with the exception of 1967 since she ascended the throne in 1952. All things apart, the Queen spends a huge amount of time travelling around the country visiting hospitals, schools, factories and other places and organizations.

3. Diana Frances Spenser, Princess of Wales (1 July 1961—31 August 1997)

Diana, Princess of Wales, is the most adored and also one of the most controversial figures of British Royalty.

Diana Frances Spencer was born into a family of British nobility, Spenser family. She

had four siblings and her parents divorced when she was only seven. She received education primarily in England and Switzerland. After graduation, Diana took up a handful of low-paying jobs such as a dance instructor for youth, a playgroup preschool assistant, and a nanny for an American family who were living in London then.

Diana came to prominence in February 1981 when her engagement to Prince Charles was announced and she lived in the limelight ever since. Her wedding to Prince of Wales was held at St. Paul's Cathedral on 29 July 1981 and broadcast live on television; globally over 750 million audiences tuned in to watch the wedding of the century. Their marriage resulted in two sons—respectively William in June 1982 and Harry in September 1984, who were second and third in the line of succession to the British throne then. She made every effort to help the two princes live a normal life as much as possible.

As Princess of Wales, Diana undertook royal duties on behalf of the Queen and represented her at functions overseas as well. Apart from the royal duties, she was honored and remembered for her dedication to charity. She carried out 191 official engagements in 1988 and 397 in 1991. She worked with patients with AIDS and leprosy(麻风病).

Unfortunately, the fairy tale wedding of Princess Diana and Prince Charles did not come to a happily-ever-after marriage. The couple was estranged and their marriage came to an end in 1996. After the divorce, Diana maintained a high level of popularity for her devotion to the two young princes and her charitable efforts. Her excessive exposure to the mass media also brought her an irrevocable mistake: Her romance with Dodi Fayed caused a stir and created media frenzy. She was fatally injured in a car crash and died the following day when escaping from the paparazzi(狗仔队).

4. Tony Blair (6 May 1953—)

Anthony Charles Lynton Blair, or Tony Blair as he is commonly called, is the Prime Minister of the UK from 1997 to 2007 and Leader of the Labor Party from 1994 to 2007.

Tony Blair was born and raised chiefly in Edinburg, Scotland. He moved with his parents and elder brother to Adelaide, Australia where his younger sister was born. Four

Unit Six   British Royalty

years later, they moved back. Young Blair seemed to have an enthusiasm for rock music. Before he enrolled in Oxford, he tried to be rock music promoter; while being a student, he played the guitar and sang in a rock band. In 1975 he graduated from Oxford with a degree of Jurisprudence and began his career from a pupil barrister, where he met his future wife. On 29 March 1980, Blair married Cherie Booth, who later became a Queen's Counsel. They have four children: Euan, Nicholas, Kathryn, and Leo.

Soon after his graduation from Oxford, Blair joined the Labor Party and was recognized as the "soft left" of the party. After repeated defeat in his early political years, Blair stood for election to the Shadow Cabinet in 1987, receiving 71 votes.

In May 1997 Blair won the general election and became the youngest Prime Minister ever since in British history. Besides, with victories in 1997, 2001, and 2005, Blair was the Labor Party's longest-serving Prime Minister, the only person to date to lead the party to three consecutive general election victories.

The Blair government sought a "Third Way" to lead Britain out of the stagnant economy. First of all, Blair made the Bank of England independent with a purpose to separate politics from economic policy. As to social policy, inequality is reduced and an emphasis on the minimum wage was put. The Blair government succeeded in limiting government spending, keeping inflation under control and reducing unemployment. Meanwhile, Blair is often severely criticized for his diplomatic policies, especially his Middle-East policy. The British Armed Forces participated in the 2001 invasion of Afghanistan and, more controversially, the 2003 invasion of Iraq. Blair also intervened militarily in Kosovo and Sierra Leone. In 2016, the Iraq Inquiry criticized his actions and described the invasion of Iraq as unjustified and unnecessary.

Ⅴ. Exercises

► **Multiple choices**: *Choose the best answer from the four choices given.*

1. So far how many queens are there in British history?
   A. Four.　　　　B. Five.　　　　C. Six.　　　　D. Seven.
2. According to their ruling time, whose reign is the shortest one?
   A. Mary Ⅰ.　　　　　　　　　B. Elizabeth Ⅰ.
   C. Mary Ⅱ.　　　　　　　　　D. Elizabeth Ⅱ.

3. Which of the following has nothing to do with constitutional monarchy?

   A. *The Bill of Rights.*   B. *Magna Carta.*

   C. *The Act of Supremacy.*   D. *The Act of Settlement* 1701.

4. Which of the following doesn't belong to the monarch's privileges?

   A. Queen can travel without a passport.

   B. Queen can refuse to pay tax.

   C. Queen can refuse to offer testimony in court.

   D. Queen can fly an airplane without a license.

5. Which statement is NOT true about Queen Elizabeth Ⅱ?

   A. She is a mother of four.

   B. She is the longest ruling monarch in the world.

   C. She joined the army in World War Ⅰ.

   D. She is the head of the UK.

6. Diana is said to be a controversial royalty. Which might not be the reason?

   A. She was born in an ordinary family.

   B. She divorced her husband, Prince Charles.

   C. She was fond of charity and helped raise funds for the underprivileged.

   D. She seemed to enjoy the limelight and accept interviews readily.

7. According to the movie *The Queen*, who has the least sympathy toward Diana?

   A. The newly-elected Prime Minister, Tony Blair.

   B. Her ex-husband, Prince Charles.

   C. Queen, her husband and her mother.

   D. The British people.

8. What is Tony Blair like in the movie *The Queen*?

   A. He is proud and arrogant towards the Royalty.

   B. He wants to modernize the Royalty eagerly.

   C. He helps the Queen out of the crisis.

   D. He is happy that Prince Charles seeks help from him and they become good friends personally.

Blank-filling: *Fill in the blanks with the missing information.*

1. Tony Blair won the Election by a _____ margin in _____ and became the _____ Prime Minister ever in British history. As it turns out, he sets a new record, and wins _____ elections in succession.

2. Diana is not a main character in the movie but she is absolutely indispensable in putting forward the plot. She mainly appears on _____ through news, reports

Unit Six British Royalty

and interviews. Her _____ is the direct _____ leading to the Royal trust crisis.

3. It is generally acknowledged that Britain prospers during the Queen's reign: _____ is the first queen in British history, and her sister _____ succeeds her as she has no offsprings. Queen Mary II and Queen Anne are also sisters. Britain becomes a world power on which "the sun never sets" during _____'s reign and _____ sets a new record of being the longest ruling queen and monarch.

4. Britain is a _____ country, where the current Queen Elizabeth II is the head of the country. Monarchy adopts hereditary system, and first three successors in line to the throne are Queen's elder son _____, her grandson _____ and her great-grandson _____.

▶ **Translate & Appreciate**: *Translate the classic lines from the movie into Chinese and share your understandings.*

1. I can see that the world has changed, and one must modernize.

   _____

   _____

2. Nowadays, people want glamour and tears, the grand performance. I'm not very good at that. I never have been. I prefer to keep my feelings to myself, and, foolishly, I believed that was what people wanted from their Queen—not to make a fuss, nor wear one's heart on one's sleeve. Duty first, self second.

   _____

   _____

   _____

3. Since last Sunday's dreadful news, we have seen, throughout Britain and around the world, an overwhelming expression of sadness at Diana's death. We have all been trying, in our different ways, to cope. It is not easy to express a sense of loss, since the initial shock is often succeeded by other feelings, disbelief, incomprehension, anger and concern for those who remain. We have all felt those emotions in these last few days, so what I say to you now, as your Queen, and as a grandmother, I say from my heart, in good times and bad… and for her devotion to her two boys. Millions who never met her, but felt they knew her, will remember her. I, for one, believe there are lessons to be drawn from her life, and from the extraordinary and moving reaction to her death. I share in your

determination to cherish her memory. I hope that, tomorrow, we can all, wherever we are, join in expressing our grief at Diana's loss and gratitude for her all-too-short life. May those who died rest in peace, and may we, each and every one of us, thank God for someone who made many, many people happy.

_____
_____
_____
_____
_____
_____

VI. Critical Thinking

1. According to the survey, 70% or up to three fourths of the Britons love Elizabeth II and the constitutional monarchy. Is this political system duplicable? Justify your points.

2. One man's meat is another man's poison. Diana, in the eyes of the Royalty, was a black sheep—disobedient, rebellious and daring. Can you explain the popularity of Diana among the ordinary publics?

Unit Six   British Royalty

Section B   The King's Speech

> If I am King, where is my power? Can I declare war? Form a government? Levy a tax? No! And yet I am the seat of all authority because they think that when I speak, I speak for them. But I can't speak.
>
> —George VI in The King's Speech

I. Warm-up Questions

1. Is eloquence important to the monarch? Why or why not?
2. How does the British Royalty select the future king or queen?
3. Edward VIII is the only British sovereign to abdicate voluntarily. Do you know the reason?

II. Basics about the Movie

Genre: drama, history
Director: Tom Hooper
Starring: Colin Firth
　　　　　Geoffrey Rush
　　　　　Helena Bonham Carter
Release Year: 2011
Running Time: 119 minutes
Country: the UK

III. Synopsis

Based on the true story of the Queen of England's father and his remarkable friendship with maverick Australian speech therapist Lionel Logue, the movie tells the story of King George VI of his impromptu ascension to the throne and the speech therapist who helped the unsure monarch make his first wartime radio broadcast on Britain's declaration of war against Germany in 1939.

Prince Albert stammers through his speech closing the British Empire Exhibition at Wembley Stadium. The Duke has given up hope of a cure, but his wife Elizabeth persuades him to see an Australian speech therapist, Lionel Logue. Misunderstandings ensue at their first meeting. King George V also demands Albert to train himself by reading the King's speech but it turns  into a failure. Albert turns to the therapist and shares some of his secrets with him and they two become friends.

Prince David ascends the throne as King Edward VIII after the death of his father King George V, but his romance with a married American woman Wallis Simpson leads to a constitutional crisis and in order to marry her, King Edward VIII abdicates the throne within a year. Albert reluctantly succeeds his brother as the new king.

During this troubled time, the misunderstanding between Albert and Logue deepens. Stimulated by Logue's disrespect, Albert surprisingly bursts out words of outrage eloquently and finally allows Logue to rehearse him for the upcoming coronation ceremony.

Upon Britain's declaration of World War II against Nazi Germany in 1939, King George VI summons Logue to Buckingham Palace to prepare for his upcoming radio address to Britain and the Empire. At this critical moment, the Archbishop of Canterbury, Winston Churchill and Prime Minister Neville Chamberlain are  present to offer support and King George VI does deliver his speech smoothly.

IV. Culture Links

1. The Act of Settlement 1701 (《王位继承法》1701)

The United Kingdom is a constitutional monarchy: succession to the British throne is hereditary. The Glorious Revolution of 1688 led to a constitutional monarchy restricted by laws such as *The Bill of Rights* 1689 (《权利法案》1689) and *The Act of Settlement* 1701.

Unit Six British Royalty

The Act of Settlement is an act of the Parliament of England, originally filed in 1700, and passed in 1701, to settle the succession to the English throne on the Electress Sophia of Hanover—a granddaughter of James I—and her Protestant heirs. Along with the Bill of Rights 1689, it remains today one of the main constitutional laws governing the succession to the throne of the United Kingdom, as well as the other Commonwealth Realm.

The act was prompted by the failure of King William III and Queen Mary II, as well as of Mary's sister Queen Anne, to produce any surviving children, and the Roman Catholic religion of all other members of the House of Stuart. In accordance with the Act of Settlement, those who were Roman Catholics, and those who married Roman Catholics, were barred from ascending the throne. The act also placed limits on both the role of foreigners in the British government and the power of the monarch with respect to the Parliament of England.

Some of those provisions have been altered by subsequent legislation. In 2011, the 16 leaders from Commonwealth countries voted unanimously to alter the centuries' old rule of succession to include daughters as well as sons. Previously, daughters could only inherit the British throne if there were no living sons. Another age-old rule that was also tossed out in 2011 stipulated that no heir could assume the throne if he or she were married to a Roman Catholic.

Since days of ancient times, the royal line of succession to the British throne was—like in most monarchies—based on primogeniture (长子继承权), which traditionally gives preference to the firstborn male heir of a king and queen, meaning he inherits the title, lands and all other property belonging to his family.

Nowadays, in most cases all male and female heirs are provided with some share or lands, titles or other rewards, even if they don't inherit a royal crown.

2. George V and His Sons

George V (George Frederick Ernest Albert) was born on 3 June 1865 in London, the second son of the Prince of Wales (Edward VII) and grandson of Queen Victoria. George served in the Royal Navy for 12 years until the unexpected death of his elder brother in early 1892 which put him directly in line for the throne. He succeeded his father in 1910 as George V. George V married his brother's fiancée and they had five sons and one daughter.

Public respect for the King increased during World War I, when George V made many visits to the front line, hospitals, factories and dockyards. In 1917 anti-German feeling led him to adopt the family name of Windsor, replacing the Germanic Saxe-Coburg-Gotha. He embodied diligence and duty and sought to represent his subjects, rather than define government policy, as his predecessors Victoria and Edward had. He died on 20 January 1936 and was succeeded by his son Edward.

Edward Ⅷ (Edward Albert Christian George Andrew Patrick David) was born on 23 June 1894, the eldest son of George Ⅴ and Queen Mary. The only British sovereign to abdicate voluntarily, Edward stepped down in 1936 to marry the American divorcee Wallis Simpson. He was King for less than a year.

As a young man, Edward Ⅷ and his brother Albert served in the British Army during World War Ⅰ and he also undertook several overseas tours on behalf of his father. The year 1936 witnessed the death of King George Ⅴ, as well as the new King Edward Ⅷ's ascending and abdicating the throne respectively at the beginning and end of the year.

Edward Ⅷ had affairs with a number of married women in the 1920s, but then met and fell in love with Wallis Simpson, the wife of an American businessman. A divorced woman with two living ex-husbands was politically and socially unacceptable as a prospective queen consort. Additionally, such a marriage would have conflicted with Edward's status as the titular head of the Church of England, which at the time disapproved of remarriage after divorce if a former spouse was still alive. Edward Ⅷ chose to abdicate when he found it impossible to marry Wallis Simpson and remain on the throne at the same time. With a reign of 326 days, Edward is one of the shortest-reigning monarchs in British history.

George Ⅵ (Albert Frederick Arthur George), the second son of George Ⅴ, is named after his great-grandfather, Albert, Prince Consort. Initially, as the second son of the King, he was not expected to inherit the throne, so he spent his early years in the navy and attended World War Ⅰ. In 1920, Albert was made the Duke of York; in 1923, he married Lady Elizabeth Bowes-Lyon, a girl not of royal birth and they had two daughters, Elizabeth and Margaret. Albert also suffered from stammer and received therapy in the mid-1920s, which is the theme of the movie *The King's Speech*.

The year 1936 witnessed the death of King George Ⅴ and the abdication of King Edward Ⅷ. Albert was forced to ascend the throne as the third monarch of the House of Windsor. During his reign, the British Empire broke up and transited into the Commonwealth Nations.

Unit Six British Royalty

The United Kingdom was also involved in World War II. During this period, Gorge VI made friends with the then Prime Minister Winston Churchill, and their friendship was called "the closest personal relationship in modern British history between a monarch and a Prime Minister".

The stress of the war had taken its toll on the King's health; besides, Gorge VI was a heavy smoker and developed lung cancer among others. In 1952 George VI was found dead in his sleep at the age of 56. Shortly after, his elder daughter Elizabeth ascended the throne as Elizabeth II.

▶ 3. British Monarchs and Their Nicknames

It seems impossible to remember the names of British monarchs and their sequence of sovereign correctly because since Norman Conquest in 1066, there lived 41 monarchs in Britain, including 8 Edwards, 8 Henrys, 6 Georges, 4 Williams, 3 Richards, 2 Charles, 2 Marys, 2 Elizabeths, and 2 James. The Westerns have a preference for naming their children either after the saints or their grandparents. British monarch's nicknames, in this way, may help to memorize who is who.

◇ King William I / *Willam the Conqueror* (1028—1087)　　"征服者"威廉
◇ William Rufus / *William the Red* (1056—1100)　　"红毛王"威廉
◇ Henry I / *Henry Beauclerc* (1068—1135)　　"好学者"亨利一世
◇ Richard I / *Richard the Lionheart* (1157—1199)　　"狮心王"理查
◇ King John / *John Lackland* (1166—1216)　　"无地王"约翰
◇ Edward I / *Edward Longshanks* (1239—1307)　　"长腿"爱德华
◇ Mary I / *Bloody Mary* (1516—1558)　　"血腥玛丽"
◇ Elizabeth I / *Queen of Virgin* (1533—1603)　　"童贞"女王

V. **Exercises**

▶ **True or False Statements**: *Read the following statements and decide whether they are true (T) or false (F).*

　　_____1. The British Royalty selects the new king or queen according to the will of the old monarch.

　　_____2. The British monarch has the responsibility of delivering speeches on different occasions.

　　_____3. *The Act of Settlement* 1701 is out of date and has been abolished.

　　_____4. Edward VIII is the shortest reigning king in British history.

123

_____ 5. George Ⅴ is the father of George Ⅳ, brother of Edward Ⅷ.

_____ 6. The king's or queen's marriage is usually arranged by the Royalty family and the king or queen has no right to choose a future spouse.

_____ 7. It is not uncommon for the Royal cousins to get married, such as Queen Victoria and Prince Albert, Queen Elizabeth Ⅱ and Prince Philip.

_____ 8. George Ⅵ replaced his brother to be the British King because his brother was determined to marry a Roman Catholic, which was unacceptable to the Royalty.

_____ 9. Richard Ⅰ is also called Richard the Lionheart because he was as brave as a lion in the battlefield.

_____ 10. *The King's Speech* is based on the true story of British King, George Ⅵ.

Short-answer Questions: *Give brief answers to the following questions.*

1. How does the British Royalty choose the future monarch?

   _____

2. What's the relationship between the Windsor monarchs?

   _____

3. According to the movie, how does George Ⅵ overcome his stammering?

   _____

Extracurricular Exploration: *Explore the Internet. Find out the answers to the following questions and make a no-more-than-5-minute presentation.*

1. Introduce one of the kings or queens in British history and explain how his nickname came into being, if any.

2. Elizabeth Ⅱ has a big family—3 sons and 1 daughter, 8 grandchildren and at least 5 great-grandchildren and she has entered her nineties. Can you list the line of succession in Britain?

Unit Six British Royalty

Section C Henry VIII (2003)

I. Movie Information (Explore and Find)

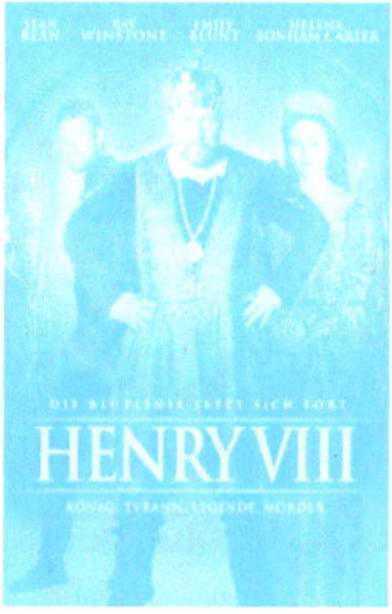

Genre: _____
Chinese Title: _____
Director: _____
Starring: _____
Running Time: _____ minutes
Release Year: 2003
Country: _____

► Use the information you have found to fill in the blanks.

Henry VIII (2003) is a(n) _____ (country) _____ (genre) two-part TV serial documenting the stormy-year (1509—1547) reign of King Henry VIII, from the disintegration of his first marriage to an aging Spanish princess until his death following a stroke in 1547.

Henry VIII is one of the most famous kings in English history. He was the second _____ monarch and was well-known for his _____ marriages in his search for political alliance, marital bliss and a healthy male heir. His break with the papacy in Rome established the _____ and began _____. Three of his children became the King or Queen in history. They were respectively _____, _____, and _____.

II. Synopsis

The two-part TV movie chronicles the life of Henry VIII of England from the disintegration of his first marriage to his death following a stroke in 1547, by which time he had married for the sixth time.

The first episode begins with the dying old King, Henry VII, who implores his heir, Henry Tudor, to marry his brother's widow and have a son to secure the family line.

Fifteen years later, Henry Ⅷ becomes the greatest King ever. Unfortunately, the King and Queen don't have a son; the couple only has a daughter Mary survived. The King is attracted by a girl called Anne Boleyn and he uses his power to cancel the marriage between Anne and her fiancé. Resolving that Anne will become his wife instead of his mistress, the King instructs his chancellor to find out a way to annul his marriage with the Queen, which leads to his break with the Catholic Church. Later, Anne delivers a princess, Elizabeth and his ardor towards her fades out. Anne gets pregnant once again and succeeds in giving birth to a son after the premature labor. The first episode ends with the King trying to get rid of Anne.

The second episode starts with Jane Seymour being dressed for her wedding and her subsequent introduction to the people who take her to their hearts, whilst the King and Cromwell differ on the dissolution of the monasteries which have angered the English Catholics and united them into a huge army to march on London in protest. Much to Henry's joy, the Queen gives birth to a prince and the joy soon turns into grief with the death of the Queen soon after the labor. Henry marries Anne of Cleves, and Catherine Howard. Young Catherine is beheaded just like her cousin, Anne Boleyn. With the demise of Catholic peers the reformers take the opportunity to consolidate their powers, enhanced by the wedding of the King to Catherine Parr who attempts to unite the royal family. The film closes as the King reflects on his past loves.

Ⅲ. Culture Links

▶ 1. Henry Ⅷ and the English Reformation

Henry Tudor, son of Henry Ⅶ of England and Elizabeth York, was born at the royal residence, Greenwich Palace, on June 28, 1491. Following the death of his father, he became Henry Ⅷ, King of England. He married six times, beheaded two of his wives and was the main instigator of the English Reformation. His only surviving son, Edward Ⅵ, succeeded him after his death on January 28, 1547.

The English Reformation was a series of events initiated in the 16th century England by which the Church of England broke away from the authority of the Pope and the Roman Catholic Church. Despite the zeal of religious reformers in Europe, England was slow to question the established Church. During the reign of Henry Ⅷ, however, the tide turned in favour of Protestantism, and by the 1600s the new Church held sway over the old.

The progress of the Reformation in England was closely bound up with Henry's personal affairs. In his first marriage with the widow of his brother, Henry Ⅷ only had one daughter and he claimed that the lack of a male heir was due to the invalid marriage; therefore, he asked the Pope to annul the marriage, which was refused due to the fact that earlier that year the nephew of the Queen, the Emperor of Rome briefly took the Pope into prison. The Pope was afraid to offend the powerful ruler of Rome. In 1532, Henry Ⅷ took matters into his own hands by declaring the church in England should separate from the church in Rome. In his reign, Henry Ⅷ succeeded in separating the Anglican Church from the Roman hierarchy, the Dissolution of the Monasteries, and establishing himself as the Supreme Head of the Church of England. Since him, the British monarchs are all the Head of the Church of England.

2. Henry Ⅷ and His Wives

Henry Ⅷ was not originally meant to be King. His elder brother Arthur died when Henry was 12. He became the King of England after his father died in 1509. As the King, he had to marry his brother's widow, Spanish Princess **Katherine of Aragon** as his wife as the country needed stability and a male heir. Unfortunately, they only had one daughter survived. When his request for the Pope to annul his marriage failed, he broke up with the Church and married the then pregnant **Anne Boleyn** secretly, which made him father of another girl. His third marriage finally produced the son he so desperately desired in 1537 but the Queen **Jane Seymour** died 12 days after the childbirth. His fourth marriage with German Princess **Anne of Cleves** only lasted for 6 months. In 1540, the aging King married the teenage **Catherine Howard**. Their marriage was short-lived too. Henry's final marriage to **Catherine Parr**, who acted like a nurse, was more harmonious and she would go on to outlive him. Henry died in London at the age of 56 with his son and the sixth wife both at his side.

3. Contributions of Henry Ⅷ

Notable events during his reign included the break with Rome and the subsequent establishment of the independent Church of England, the Dissolution of the Monasteries, and the union of England and Wales.

Several significant pieces of legislation were enacted during Henry Ⅷ's reign. They included several Acts which severed the English Church from the Roman Catholic Church and established Henry as the Supreme Head of the Church in England.

Henry was an avid gambler and dice player, and as well, an accomplished musician, author, poet, and sportsman. He was also involved in the construction and improvement of several buildings, including King's College, Cambridge; Christ Church, Oxford; Hampton Court Palace, Nonsuch Palace, and Westminster Abbey. His sponsorship of education and arts contributed to the English Renaissance which continued under the reign of his daughter, Elizabeth Ⅰ.

His enduring legacy is the start of the English Reformation, initially triggered not by theological but political reasons. As a result of the church-state relationship that emerged under Henry Ⅷ (with the King as Head of the Church, following Martin Luther's model) and of efforts to impose membership of the Church of England on the whole population, other denominations evolved during the years that followed Henry's reign.

Ⅳ. Expansion

Henry Ⅷ is a hot figure in literature and the movie world because he is a man of many things: an avid gambler and dice player, and as well, an accomplished musician, author, poet, and sportsman. His love affairs and six wives are much discussed in movies such as *The Private Life of Henry Ⅷ* (1933), *Anne of the Thousand Days* (1969), *Henry the Eighth and His Six Wives* (1972), and *The Other Boleyn Girl* (2008). Fill in the blanks with the information given above and see whether you can have any findings.

Wives of Henry Ⅷ	Name	Give Birth to Any Prince or Princess	Personal Destiny	Anything Particular
1st				
2nd				
3rd				
4th				
5th				
6th				

V. Fun Time

Queen Elizabeth II delivered her first Christmas speech on TV in 1957 and since then in the following years to make an annual Christmas speech has become a tradition. The Queen also delivers speeches on such occasions as Accession Anniversary, the Commonwealth Day, State Opening of Parliament, etc. Besides, Queen's Received Pronunciation (RP) English draws fans worldwide.

The theme of Christmas speech is varied and before the speech the British National Anthem *God Bless the Queen* is usually played. Let's listen to one of the Queen's Christmas speeches and find out its theme and key points.

Theme: _____

Key points: _____

_____

_____

_____

Unit Seven

Legends

Section A King Arthur
Section B Robin Hood: Prince of Thieves
Section C The Pursuit of D.B. Cooper

Preface

Legends are stories about supernatural or mythical people or events written in history, which often convey a lesson or moral and are narrated to retain the values that are part of the community. Legends may be different from myths but both are passed down from one generation to another orally or through the written medium.

This unit focuses on three legendary figures in history: Section A is entitled King Arthur, a legendary king who led the defence of Britain against Saxon invaders in the late 5th and early 6th centuries AD; Section B *Robin Hood: Prince of Thieves*, a movie about how an English young man Robin fought back the tyranny and chose to be an outlaw in the 13th century; D. B. Cooper is a mysterious 1971 American hijacker, who had been on the list of pursuit by the FBI until 2016.

Unit Goals

- To have a deep understanding of the historical background of these legends;
- To have a basic understanding of the lessons or morals conveyed in these legends;
- To be able to distinguish legends from myths.

Unit Seven Legends

Section A   King Arthur

> Merciful God, I have such need of your mercy now. Not for myself, but for my knights, for they are truly in need of you. Deliver them from their trial ahead and I will repay you a thousand fold with any sacrifices you've asked me.
>
> —King Arthur in *King Arthur*

 I. Warm-up Questions

1. Can you talk about Roman's invasion into Britain and their influence on the contemporary Britain?

2. King Arthur is a legendary figure in British history. Can you name a few any other figures like him in British history?

3. The road to freedom can never be easy. How do you define the leading function of the legendary figure in history?

 II. Basics about the Movie

Genre: legend
Director: Antoine Fuqua
Starring: Clive Owen
　　　　　Stephen Dillane
　　　　　Keira Knightley
Release Year: 2004
Running Time: 126 minutes
Country: the USA, Ireland, the UK

III. Synopsis

This original portrayal of Arthur, as opposed to the mystical elements of the tale in past Arthur films, uses names and other elements from the traditional, medieval, Catholic Arthurian cycle in a very different, yet historically less implausible, almost realistic plot.

Around 400 AD, the Roman Empire is stretched across many nations, including Britain. In their conquest for more land, the Romans went into Sarmatia where they fought against the very brave Sarmatian cavalry. The Romans, impressed by the Sarmatians' weaponry and fighting skills, included them into their army as knights. After 15 years of serving and fighting for the Roman Empire the Sarmatian Knights, led by Arthur, are about to receive their freedom as the Romans are leaving Britain. But the Knights must carry out one final order before they are free. A Roman priest and his family, especially his son Alecto, must be rescued from the invading Saxons. But there is another danger lurking on the road to freedom—the Woads, British rebels who hate the Romans, led by the magician Merlin, who however realizes Rome is no longer the main threat and offers Artorius a novel alliance after sparing his life in an ambush.

Arthur is grief-stricken over Lancelot's death and says he has let them all down, but the survivors—Gawain, Galahad, and Bors—stand by him. In the final scene, Merlin marries Arthur and Guinevere and Arthur is proclaimed King to the joy and support of the Woads and Knights alike.

IV. Culture Links

1. King Arthur

King Arthur is a legendary king of Britain. He is also a legendary British leader who, according to medieval histories and romances, led the defense of Britain against Saxon invaders in the late 5th and early 6th centuries AD. The details of Arthur's story are mainly composed of folklore and literary invention, and his historical existence is debated and disputed by modern historians. The sparse historical background of Arthur is gleaned from various sources, including *the Annales Cambriae* (Latin for *The Annals of Wales*), *the Historia Brittonum* (Latin for *The*

History of the Britons), and the writings of Gildas. Arthur's name also occurs in early poetic sources such as Y Gododdin.

Arthur is a central figure in the legends making up the Matter of Britain. The legendary Arthur developed as a figure of international interest largely through the popularity of Geoffrey of Monmouth's fanciful and imaginative 12th-century history of the kings of Britain. In some Welsh and Breton tales and poems previous to this work, Arthur appears either as a great warrior defending Britain from human and supernatural enemies or as a magical figure of folklore, sometimes associated with the Welsh Otherworld, Annwn. How much of Geoffrey's Historia (completed in 1138) was adapted from such earlier sources, rather than invented by Geoffrey himself, is unknown.

Although the themes, events and characters of the Arthurian legend varied widely from text to text, and there is no canonical version, Geoffrey's version of events often served as the starting point for later stories. Geoffrey depicted Arthur as a king of Britain who defeated the Saxons and established an empire over Britain, Ireland, Iceland, Norway and Gaul. Many elements and incidents that are now an integral part of the Arthurian story appear in Geoffrey's Historia, including Arthur's father Uther Pendragon, the wizard Merlin, Arthur's wife Guinevere, the sword Excalibur, Arthur's conception at Tintagel, his final battle against Mordred at Camlann, and final rest in Avalon. The 12th-century French writer Chrétien de Troyes, who added Lancelot and the Holy Grail(圣杯) to the story, began the genre of Arthurian romance that became a significant strand of medieval literature. In these French stories, the narrative focus often shifts from King Arthur himself to other characters, such as various Knights of the Round Table. Arthurian literature thrived during the Middle Ages but waned in the centuries that followed until it experienced a major resurgence in the 19th century. In the 21st century, the legend lives on, not only in literature but also in adaptations for theatre, film, television, comics and other media.

2. Roman's Invasion into Britain

Recorded history in Britain began in the year 55 BC, when Julius Caesar(凯撒大帝, 100 BC—44 BC) and his Roman troops invaded the island. British history before that time is largely undocumented. In 55 BC and 54 BC, Britain was twice invaded by Roman troops led by Julius Caesar and was invaded again by the Romans under Claudius I in 43 AD. Britain subsequently

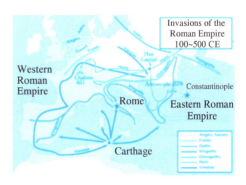

became a Roman province and remained so until the beginning of the 5th century. Many of the native Celts were driven to the mountainous regions of Scotland and Wales, which remained unconquered by the Romans. The Romans constructed towns and cities which prospered far longer than any previous settlements on the island.

In 410, German barbarians attacked Rome, forcing all Roman troops to leave Britain in order to defend their own nation, and thus ending the Roman occupation of the island.

3. Anglo-Saxon's Invasion in Britain

Soon after the Romans left, the Anglos, the Saxons and the Jutes landed in Britain. They drove the Britons to the mountains, and those that did not flee remained as slaves to the new invaders. The Anglos settled in East Anglia, the midlands and the North, the Saxons in the South and Midlands, and the Jutes in the South and Southeast. From that time on, English replaced the old Celtic language as the dominant language of the land. The country became known as England, meaning "the land of the Anglos".

The Anglo-Saxons were not Roman Christians when they went to Britain. By order of Pope Gregory Ⅰ(格列高利一世), St. Augustine(圣奥古斯丁) was sent to Britain to convert the Anglo-Saxons. St. Augustine arrived in Kent in 597 with 40 missionaries(传教士). They completed their task smoothly and converted many Anglo-Saxons to Roman Christianity. By the late 7th century, Roman Christianity became the dominant religion in Britain.

4. The Knights of Round Table

The Knights of Round Table were characters in the legends about King Arthur. They were the best knights in King Arthur's kingdom, and lived in King Arthur's castle, Camelot. They were called the Knights of Round Table because of a special table in Camelot, which was round instead of rectangular. This meant that everyone who sat around it was seen as trust worthy and equal.

The Round Table Knights were a group of the greatest knights who had the honor to sit at the Round Table at King Arthur's court. According to a story, Arthur had a carpenter build the Round Table to show that no knight, not even Arthur himself was "head of the table". All were equal and the king was just "first among equals". The table was so large that it had enough seats for 1,600 men and yet could be folded up and carried on

Unit Seven Legends

horseback. According to another source, Merlin the magician had the table built for Uther, Arthur's father. Uther gave the table to King Leodegan. Later, Leodegan gave the table to Arthur after Arthur married Guenevere, Leodegan's daughter. Still another story says that the Round Table had 12 seats around it, like the table at the Last Supper, with an empty place representing Judas's seat. This seat was called the Siege Perilous, and was reserved for the knight so pure in heart that he would someday find the Holy Grail, the cup or dish used by Jesus at the Last Supper. Any other knight who sat in the seat would die. One day, Sir Galahad's name appeared on the seat. From then on, he occupied the Siege Perilous. Later, as expected, he found the Holy Grail with the other two knights.

Knights considered it a great honor to have a seat at the Round Table. Brave men came to Arthur's court from many countries hoping to become a Round Table Knight. Many stories describe the heroic deeds of various Knights of the Round Table. Several tell of the adventures of Sir Tristram and Sir Gawin. Other famous Round Table Knights included Lancelot, Bedevere, Bors, Galahad, Perceval and Modred.

The greatest adventure of the Round Table was the search for the Holy Grail. However, only the three knights—Bors, Galahad and Perceval were pure enough to be able to find the Grail. All the others had various moral defects. This fact damaged the reputation of the Round Table. To make things worse, a love affair developed between Queen Guenevere and Sir Lancelot, who was perhaps the greatest of the Round Table Knights. This scandal destroyed the bonds of respect and friendship that had united all the knights.

The mortal blow to the Round Table was given by Sir Modred, who tried to seize Arthur's power. In a battle between the forces of the two men, Arthur killed Modred but he himself was seriously wounded and soon died. The Round Table Knights broke up following the death of Arthur.

Ⅴ. Exercises

▶ **Multiple Choices**: *Choose the best answer from the four choices given.*

1. Why did Arthur hold the meeting around the big Round Table?

    A. For Equality.　　　　　　　　B. For Freedom.

    C. For convenience.　　　　　　D. Not mentioned in the film.

2. Who is Arthur's most faithful friend?

    A. A Roman priest's son Alecto.　B. Gawain.

    C. Lancelot.　　　　　　　　　D. Bors.

3. What is the Knights' final order before they are free?

    A. To drive the Saxons out of Britain.

    B. To fight against the Roman Empire.

    C. To kill all the Sarmatian cavalry.

    D. To rescue a Roman priest's son Alecto from the invading Saxons.

4. What is NOT true about King Arthur?

    A. He is a Roman officer.

    B. He is a man of chivalry.

    C. He is famous for killing his brothers.

    D. He is a legendary hero of bravery and selflessness.

5. The following statements are the descriptions of Romans in Guinevere's eyes. Which one is FALSE?

    A. They are the people who made the Britons homeless.

    B. They are the people who took what did not belong to them.

    C. They are barbarians who killed and burned.

    D. They are the wisest that helped the founding of the British nation.

6. In *King Arthur*, for what did the knights follow Arthur and fight hard?

    A. For going back quickly to Rome.

    B. For national unification of Great Britain.

    C. For independence and freedom.

    D. For their loyalty to Great Britain.

Unit Seven Legends

- **Blank-filling**: *Fill in the blanks with the missing information.*

  1. King Arthur is a _____ British leader who, according to the medieval histories and romances, led the defense of Britain against _____ invaders in the late 5th and early 6th centuries AD.

  2. Arthur was the first born son of King Uther Pendragon and _____ to the throne. However these were very troubled times and Merlin, a wise _____, advised that the baby Arthur should be raised in a secret place and that none should know his true identity. Merlin used his magic to set a sword in a stone. Written on the sword, in letters of gold, were these words: "Whoso pullet out this sword of this stone is the rightwise born king of all _____." Arthur, quite by chance, withdrew the sword.

  3. In the early 19th century, _____, _____, and the _____ reawakened interest in Arthur and the medieval romances. A new code of ethics for 19th-century gentlemen was shaped around the _____ ideals embodied in the "Arthur of romance". In recent years the portrayal of Arthur as a real hero of the 5th century has also made its way into film versions of the Arthurian legend, most notably the TV series' _____ (1972—1973), _____ (2008—2012), _____ (1979), and _____ (2011) and the feature films _____ (2004), _____(2007) and _____ (2017).

  4. Historians agree that the classical 15th century tale of King Arthur and his _____ rose from a real hero who lived a thousand years earlier in a period often called the _____ Ages.

  5. In the history of Europe, the Middle Ages or Medieval Period lasted from the _____ to the _____ century.

- **Translate & Appreciate**: *Translate the classic lines from the movie into Chinese and share your understandings.*

  1. Arthur, this is not for Roman fight, it is not your own fight, all these long years we've been together, the trials we faced, the blood we shed, what it's all for if it's not for the reward of freedom, and now, we're so close, we're finally in grasp.

  _____
  _____

  2. Deeds in themselves are meaningless unless they are for some higher purpose. We have waged a war to protect a Rome that does not exist. Is that the deed I am to be judged by?

3. We are blessed and cursed by our time. What do you fear of, Arthur? You are like this country—Britain's Roman father. Roman is dead. This place, this land, your home, is the last outpost of freedom, of everything you hold dear. These are your people.

4. I don't believe in heaven. I've been living in this hell. But if you represent what heaven is, then take me there.

5. Every knight here has laid his life on the line for you, for you. And instead of freedom, you want more blood? Our blood? You think more of Roman blood than you do of ours?

▸ **Voice Your Opinion**: *Read the following two reviews about Robin Hood: Prince of Thieves. Sum up its key points and voice your opinions on this movie after you finish watching it.*

 ⟨1⟩

By Nell Minow (Common Sense Media)

Saying that this retelling of the King Arthur story is "The Truth Behind the Legend" is an overstatement of epic proportions, making the movie's tagline the only thing epic about it. The battle scenes, dialogue, and attractive actors all place *King Arthur* squarely in the realm of summer popcorn flicks: entertaining and briefly uplifting, but not destined to linger in memory, much less in history. The story sounds complicated, especially considering that it jettisons just about everything you expect in a story about King Arthur but the Round Table. It piles on the history, but there is just enough plot to fill the scenes between battles.

Those looking for the familiar terrain of King Arthur's legend—the silvery arm holding

Excalibur aloft, the search for the Grail, and the illicit love between Lancelot and Guinnevere—should head to the library. Those in search of the true stories behind King Arthur and his knights of the Round Table can look to Celtic, Scottish, Welsh, Roman, and Assyrian legends. But those looking for some memorable battle scenes and some attractive actors without too much plot to slow things down can fill up the popcorn bucket and sit back for some mindless entertainment.

Key points: _____
_____
_____
_____

 ⟨2⟩

By Kam William

King Arthur has been immortalized as the chivalrous savior of the sixth century Britain, even though he was never mentioned by name in any of the historical records or documents of the era. Nonetheless, centuries later, his alleged exploits, along with those of his famed Knights of the Round Table have remained the subject of mythmaking spun from the imagination of countless poets, troubadours, novelists, playwrights, and filmmakers. The fable has continued to tease the imagination of young and old alike, generation after generation.

In addition to honoring King Arthur, these tales of hope, courage, and honor typically feature Lady Guinevere, the magician Merlin, and noble knights such as Lancelot, Galahad, and Gawain. The legend has endured, despite the fact that leading scholars never agree on whether or not any of these characters ever actually existed.

Hollywood, which has already served up at least a dozen versions of the King Arthur story over the years, bills its latest version as "the untold true story which inspired the legend." However, the film fails to reveal the source of this newly discovered lore, other than from the imagination of sceenwriter David Franzoni who has "worked out a new approach to the subject matter." Note that in 2001, the same Mr. Franzoni was nominated for an Oscar for his original script for *Gladiator*, a work of pure fiction.

The 2004 edition of *King Arthur* was made by Antoine Fuqua, who directed MTV Award-winning rap videos before his very successful transition to feature films.

Fuqua's *King Arthur*, however, has inexplicably earned a PG-13 rating despite its savagery and sensuality. It stars Clive Owen in the title role, Ioan Gruffudd as Lancelot, Hugh Dancy as Galahad, Joel Edgerton as Gawain, and Stephen Dillane as Merlin, all of whom are overshadowed by Lady Guinevere played by Keira Knightley.

Those who may remember the chaste renditions of Guinevere delivered by Julie Andrews on Broadway and Vanessa Redgrave in the screen adaptation of *Camelot*, will be shocked by this edition. Forget the flowing, feminine silk dresses of yesteryear.

Ms. Knightley eschews them in favor of a tight-fitting leather bodice. This overhauled "Lady" is a sexy, sword wielding, arrow shooting warrior fearlessly defending the realm. She slays as many adversaries as any man in Arthur's army.

The best acting in this film is by Stellan Skarsgard, who is convincing as Cedric, the villainous lord of the Saxons. The worst is by Ray Winstone as Bors, a clown who is rolled out for a bit of comic relief every 15 minutes or so.

In many ways this movie tells us far more about the values and age in which we are living, than the one it pretends to be returning us to. Arthur is a reluctant warrior who yearns for peace. He agrees to wage a final war against the godless Saxons in order to ensure that Britain be forever Christian.

Good (2 stars). Rated PG-13 for intense battle scenes, sensuality, and profanity.

Key points: _____

_____

_____

_____

What's your impression of the movie? Write down your own ideas.

Your opinion: _____

_____

_____

_____

Unit Seven Legends

Section B   Robin Hood, the Prince of Thieves

> Then either we take our chances with the ghosts or become ghosts ourselves.
> —Robin Hood in *Robin Hood, the Prince of Thieves*

 Ⅰ. Warm-up Questions

1. What do you know about Robin Hood? And why was he called the Prince of Thieves?

2. What are the common characteristics of King Arthur and Robin Hood? And why are they the legendary figures in British history?

3. How much do you know about the dynasty of King Richard Ⅰ? And why was he called Richard the Lionheart?

 Ⅱ. Basics about the Movie

Genre: legendary, action, adventure
Director: Kevin Reynolds
Starring: Kevin Costner
Running Time: 143 minutes
Release Year: 1991
Country: the United States

 Ⅲ. Synopsis

Robin of Locksley, an English nobleman who joined Richard the Lionheart in the Third Crusade, is captured and imprisoned in Jerusalem along with his comrade Peter. Robin engineers an escape, saving the life of a Moor, Azeem in the process; Peter dies in the attempt and has Robin swear to protect his sister Marian (Mary Elizabeth

Mastrantonio). Robin returns to England with Azeem, who vows to accompany Robin until the debt of saving his life is repaid.

In England, with King Richard away, the cruel sheriff of Nottingham rules over the land, aided by his cousin, Guy of Gisbourne along with the witch Mortianna and the corrupt Bishop of Hereford. At Locksley Castle, Robin's father is lured to the gates and captured by the sheriff's men after refusing to join them.

Robin returns to England to find his father dead, his home in ruins, and the sheriff and his men oppressing the people. On his flight from the sheriff's forces, he and Azeem meet with a band of outlaws hiding in the sherwood Forest, led by Little John. Also among them is Will Scarlet, who is later revealed to be Robin's illegitimate half-brother. Robin eventually assumes command of the band, encourages his men to fight against Nottingham and trains them to defend themselves. They begin to rob English soldiers and distribute the stolen wealth among the poor. One of their early victims is Friar Tuck, who subsequently also joins the Merry Men. Robin's successes infuriate the sheriff, who increases the maltreatment of his people, resulting in more support for Robin Hood despite the sheriff's attempts to defame him and ever-growing rewards on his head.

Finally, the sheriff has had enough. Hiring Celtic warriors to bolster his forces, he tracks down the outlaws' hideout and initiates a massive attack which destroys the forest refuge. He also restrains and confines Marian when she tries to summon help from France. The sheriff proposes to Maid Marian, saying that, if she accepts, he will spare the lives of the captured woodsmen and their families. Nevertheless, several of the rebel fighters including Little John's son are to be executed by hanging.

However, despite information to the contrary, Robin and a handful of his most trusted aides did survive the assault. On the day of the sheriff and Maid Marian's wedding and the scheduled hangings, Robin and his men fight their way into Nottingham Castle and free the prisoners. The original plan was to just free their friends and retreat, but then Azeem reveals himself and his willingness to fight the sheriff, finally turning the peasants to revolt. Robin kills the sheriff, avenging his father. With his guard down, Robin is attacked by Mortianna, who charges with a spear. Azeem throws his sword, slaying Mortianna and fulfilling his vow.

Robin and Marian profess their love for one another and marry in the forest. Their wedding is briefly interrupted by the return of King Richard I, who blesses the marriage and thanks Robin for his deeds.

IV. Culture Links

1. Robin Hood

Robin Hood is a heroic outlaw in English folklore who, according to legend, is a highly skilled archer and swordsman. Traditionally depicted dressed in Lincoln green, he is said to rob the rich and give to the poor. Alongside his band of Merry Men in Sherwood Forest and against the sheriff of Nottingham, he became a popular folk figure in the late-medieval period, and continues to be widely represented in literature, film and television.

According to one legend, in the time of Richard the Lionheart a minor noble of Nottinghamshire, one Robin of Loxley, was outlawed for poaching deer. At that time the deer in a royal forest belonged to the king, and killing one of the king's deer was therefore treason, and punishable by death.

So Robin took to the greenwood of Sherwood Forest, making a living by stealing from rich travellers and distributing the loot among the poor of the area. In the process he gained a band of followers and a spouse, Maid Marian. Despite the best efforts of the evil sheriff of Nottingham he avoided capture until the return of King Richard from the Crusades brought about a full pardon and the restoration of Robin's lands. In other versions he died at the hands of a kinswoman, the abbess of Kirklees Priory.

2. King Richard I (1157—1199)

Richard I was King of England from 6 July 1189 until his death. He was the third of five sons of King Henry II of England and Duchess Eleanor of Aquitaine. He was known as Richard the Lionheart because of his reputation as a great military leader and warrior.

By the age of 16, Richard had taken command of his own army, putting down rebellions in Poitou against his father. Richard was a central Christian commander during the Third Crusade, leading the campaign after the departure of Philip II of France and scoring considerable victories against his Muslim counterpart, Saladin, although he did not retake Jerusalem from Saladin.

Richard spoke both French and Occitan①. He was born in England, where he spent his childhood; before becoming King, however, he lived most of his adult life in the Duchy of Aquitaine, in the southwest of France. Following his accession, he spent very little time, perhaps as little as six months, in England. Most of his life as King was spent on the Crusades, in captivity, or actively defending his lands in France. Rather than regarding his kingdom as a responsibility requiring his presence as ruler, he had been perceived as preferring to use it merely as a source of revenue to support his armies. Nevertheless, he was seen as a pious hero by his subjects. He remains one of the few kings of England remembered by his epithet, rather than regnal number, and is an enduring iconic figure both in England and in France.

3. The Crusades（十字军东征）

The Crusades were a series of Holy Wars launched by the Christian states of Europe against the Saracens. The term "Saracen" was the word used to describe a Moslem during the time of the Crusades. The Crusades started in 1095 when Pope Claremont preached the First Crusade at the Council of Claremont. The Pope's preaching led to thousands immediately affixing the cross to their garments—the name Crusade given to the Holy Wars came from old French word "crois" meaning "cross".

The Crusades were eight in number, the first four being sometimes called the Principal Crusades, and the remaining four the Minor Crusades. In addition there was a Children's Crusade. There were several other expeditions which were insignificant in numbers or results.

The effects of the Crusades on Europe of the Middle Ages were an important factor in the history of the progress of civilization. The effects of a Crusade influenced the wealth and power of the Catholic Church, political matters, commerce, feudalism, intellectual development, social effects, material effects and the effects of the Crusades also prompted the famous voyages of discovery.

4. Sherwood Forest

Sherwood Forest, a 450-acre country park, is located near the village of Edwinstowe in north Nottinghamshire, and the large English oak, the **Major Oak**, is thought to be between 800 and 1,000 years old. Legend has it that the ancient oak not only provided

---

① a language spoken in a region called Occitania between South France, Italy, Monaco and Spain 奥西坦语

Unit Seven Legends

Robin Hood with shelter, it was also the place where he and his Merry Men slept.

Sherwood attracts between 360,000 and 1 million tourists annually, many from other countries. Visitor number has increased significantly since the launch of the BBC's *Robin Hood* television series in 2006.

Each August the nature reserve hosts an annual, week-long Robin Hood Festival. This event recreates a medieval atmosphere and features the major characters from the Robin Hood legend.

▶ 5. Nottingham Castle

It is a historic site at the heart of the Robin Hood legend and starting point for the English Civil War. Situated on a high rock, Nottingham Castle commands spectacular views over the city and once rivaled the great castles of Windsor and the Tower of London.

Its history is chequered with sieges, murders and intrigues. Totally destroyed after the Civil War, the medieval castle was replaced by a magnificent ducal mansion in 1674. Then in 1875 it was converted into the first municipal museum and art gallery outside London. Award-winning cave tours tell this history and take you down into the passageways and tunnels beneath the building.

Ⅴ. Exercises

▶ **True or False Statements**: *Read the following statements and decide whether they are true (T) or false (F).*

　　_____ 1. Robin Hood is a heroic legendary figure in English folklore, a highly skilled archer and swordsman. He has become known for "robbing the poor and giving to the rich".

145

_____ 2. Sheriff and Bishop accuse Robin's father of murdering, before killing him.

_____ 3. Robin returns to England to find his father killed by King Richard and he vows to avenge his father's death.

_____ 4. In the film, the witch's name is Mortianna.

_____ 5. Robin Hood lives in the Black Forest and Martha is the lady he is in love with.

_____ 6. What Robin Hood once won at the Nottingham Fair is a chest of gold.

_____ 7. After Robin returns to England with Azeem, he sees Gisborne and his soldiers chasing the sheriff.

_____ 8. In many books, Robin's real name is Robin of Nottingham.

_____ 9. In England, with King Richard away, the cruel sheriff of Nottingham rules over the land, and Robin hates him most in the film.

_____ 10. Robin is a very good archer and he is famous for his sword fighting.

▶ **Short-answer Questions**: *Give brief answers to the following questions.*

1. What are the common characteristics of King Arthur and Robin Hood?

   _____

   _____

2. Why is the Middle Ages called the darkest age of all in European history?

   _____

   _____

   _____

3. In European literature, there are lots of works extolling chivalry, then what is chivalry?

   _____

   _____

   _____

4. King Arthur and Robin Hood are both legendary figures of English folktales. What ideals do they stand for the English people of that age?

   _____

   _____

   _____

Unit Seven Legends

➤ **Extracurricular Exploration**: *Explore the Internet. Find out the answers to the following questions and make a no-more-than-5-minute presentation.*

1. Surf the Internet. Find more anecdotes about Robin Hood and share them with the class.

2. Watch the movie *Robin Hood, the Prince of Thieves* to find whether there are any discrepancies between the history and the movie?

3. Find more information about the historical background of the story and illustrate why the legendary heroes like Robin Hood appeared in this period.

Section C The Pursuit of D.B. Cooper

I. Movie Information (Explore and Find)

Genre: _____
Chinese Title: _____
Director: _____
Starring: _____
Running Time: 100 minutes
Release Year: _____
Country: _____

➤ Use the information you have found to fill in the blanks.

The Pursuit of D. B. Cooper is a _____ (year) _____ (country) _____ (genre) film about an actual infamous aircraft hijacker _____, who escaped with $200,000 after leaping from the back of a _____ airliner on November 24, 1971. The bulk of the film fictionalizes Cooper's escape after he landed on the ground. Although his fate and whereabouts have remained a _____, this story speculates about what may have happened.

The film is based on the American poet J. D. Reed's 1980 novel _____. The film almost never got finished. The change in directors led to numerous re-shoots and obvious continuity problems with the finished product. In an attempt to drum up publicity for the film, _____ offered a million-dollar-reward for any information that would lead to the capture and arrest of the real D. B. Cooper. No one ever claimed the money.

The Pursuit of D. B. Cooper, although similar to other hijacking films of the period, was not a _____ at the box office. In a critical review of the film, Vincent Canby in his assessment for *The New York Times*, succinctly noted that: "… a number of excellent actors into performing what is dismally unfunny chase-comedy that eventually seems as aimless, shortsighted and cheerlessly cute as the character they've made up and called 'D. B. Cooper'." Roger Spottiswoode, however, would win the _____ Prize in 1982.

Unit Seven   Legends

Ⅱ. Synopsis

In 1971, a hijacker, identified as "D. B. Cooper", jumps from an airliner using by the rear exit. He jumps on a clear day, parachuting into a forest in Washington State. The man is later identified as Jim Meade, an ex-Army man with big dreams. Meade escapes the manhunt using a Jeep he had previously hidden in the forest and concealing the money in the carcass of a deer. He eventually meets up with his estranged wife Hannah, who operates a river rafting company. Meanwhile, Meade is being hunted by Bill Gruen, an insurance investigator who was Meade's sergeant in the Army, and Meade's Army buddy, Remson, who remembered Meade talking about hijacking an aircraft.

Gruen confronts the Meades at the rafting company, but they escape down the river. The Meades lead Gruen and Remson on a cross-country chase involving various stolen cars. Gruen is fired by his employer, but continues the chase to claim the money for himself. At the aircraft boneyard near Tucson, Arizona, the Meades acquire a hot-air balloon, but Gruen steals the money from Hannah. Meade chases him down with a barely functioning Boeing-Stearman PT-17 crop duster biplane. Meade runs Gruen off the road but crashes his aircraft.

Recovering from the wrecks, Meade has Gruen's gun and for a few minutes, they discuss how Gruen knew that Meade was D. B. Cooper. Along with clues he had left, the previous encounters between the two men in the Army had convinced Gruen that only Meade could have pulled off the audacious hijacking.

Meade leaves Gruen with a couple bundles of the cash, and walks away with the rest, to be picked up by Hannah. With Gruen abandoning the pursuit, it is up to Remson to try to recover the stolen money. When he reaches a crossroads the Meades have just passed, thinking he sees their truck parked nearby, Remson continues the chase.

Ⅲ. Culture Links

1. About D. B. Cooper

D. B. Cooper is a media epithet popularly used to refer to a hijacker of a Boeing 727 aircraft in Washington, on November 24, 1971. He parachuted from the plane with a ransom over a million dollars at current values. That law enforcement would record the serial numbers of ransom money and trace the perpetrators when they spent it had been known to the American public since the trial following the Lindbergh kidnapping. There has been some speculation that Cooper's motive was thrill seeking or a grudge rather than financial as he could hardly have expected to ever spend the actual ransom or even safely fence it at a discount. Cooper possessed knowledge that was virtually unique to paramilitary units of CIA, but his parachuting skills were questionable. He avoided detection from an air force jet escort by leaving the plane while it was passing through a storm, which experts considered very dangerous. He is believed to have come down in a wilderness area. Despite an exhaustive FBI investigation, his fate remains uncertain. None of the money was ever used.

The FBI officially suspended active investigation of the case in July 2016, but continues to request that any physical evidence that might emerge related to the parachutes or the ransom money be submitted for analysis.

2. More Airplane-hijacking

Do you know other hijackings in recent years? Please fill in the missing information.

1. **Hijackers'/Hijacker's Name(s):** _____
   When it happened: _____
   Where it happened: _____
   For what: _____
   Casualty: _____
   Influence: _____

2. **Hijackers'/Hijacker's Name(s):** _____
   When it happened: _____
   Where it happened: _____
   For what: _____
   Casualty: _____
   Influence: _____

Unit Seven Legends

 IV. **Expansion**

In this movie, D. B. Cooper seems to possess the knowledge that was actually unique to paramilitary units of CIA. CIA and FBI, as two top and the most important information bureaus, are both often mentioned in the film. Can you assort them out and finish the table?

	CIA	FBI
Formed		
Motto		
Stand for		
Headquarters		
Employees		
Website		
Annual Budget		
Agency Executives		
Missions & Functions		
Organizational Structure		
Joining Qualifications		

Ⅴ. Fun Time

Watch George W. Bush's 9.11 address to the nation delivered on 11 September, Oval Office, Washington, D. C. In the speech, Bush said: "A great people has been moved to defend a great nation…"

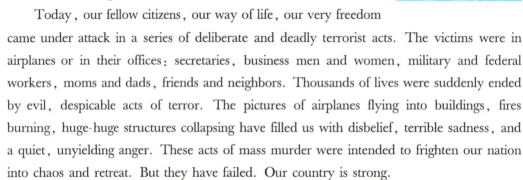

This 599-word Address tolls the bells of fighting back the terrorism worldwide. It goes like this:

Good evening,

Today, our fellow citizens, our way of life, our very freedom came under attack in a series of deliberate and deadly terrorist acts. The victims were in airplanes or in their offices: secretaries, business men and women, military and federal workers, moms and dads, friends and neighbors. Thousands of lives were suddenly ended by evil, despicable acts of terror. The pictures of airplanes flying into buildings, fires burning, huge-huge structures collapsing have filled us with disbelief, terrible sadness, and a quiet, unyielding anger. These acts of mass murder were intended to frighten our nation into chaos and retreat. But they have failed. Our country is strong.

A great people has been moved to defend a great nation. Terrorist attacks can shake the foundations of our biggest buildings, but they cannot touch the foundation of America. These acts shatter steel, but they cannot dent the steel of American resolve. America was targeted for attack because we're the brightest beacon for freedom and opportunity in the world. And no one will keep that light from shining. Today, our nation saw evil—the very worst of human nature—and we responded with the best of America. With the daring of our rescue workers, with the caring for strangers and neighbors who came to give blood and help in any way they could.

Immediately following the first attack, I implemented our government's emergency response plans. Our military is powerful, and it's prepared. Our emergency teams are working in New York City and Washington D. C. to help with local rescue efforts. Our first priority is to get help to those who have been injured, and to take every precaution to protect our citizens at home and around the world from further attacks. The functions of our government continue without interruption. Federal agencies in Washington which had to be evacuated today are reopening for essential personnel tonight and will be open for business tomorrow. Our financial institutions remain strong, and the American economy will be open for business as well.

The search is underway for those who were behind these evil acts. I have directed the full resources of our intelligence and law enforcement communities to find those responsible and to bring them to justice. We will make no distinction between the terrorists who committed these acts and those who harbor them.

I appreciate so very much the members of Congress who have joined me in strongly condemning these attacks. And on behalf of the American people, I thank the many world leaders who have called to offer their condolences and assistance. America and our friends and allies join with all those who want peace and security in the world, and we stand together to win the war against terrorism.

Tonight, I ask for your prayers for all those who grieve, for the children whose worlds have been shattered, for all whose sense of safety and security has been threatened. And I pray they will be comforted by a power greater than any of us, spoken through the ages in Psalm 23:

Even though I walk through the valley of the shadow of death, I fear no evil for you are with me.

This is a day when all Americans from every walk of life unite in our resolve for justice and peace. America has stood down enemies before, and we will do so this time. None of us will ever forget this day, yet we go forward to defend freedom and all that is good and just in our world.

Thank you. Good night. And God bless America.

Unit Eight

Literature

Section A   Pride and Prejudice
Section B   Gone with the Wind
Section C   For Whom the Bell Tolls

Preface

Literature works are the wealth of mankind. English literature is a rich ore for ESL learners to exploit. The vitality of classic literature lies in its flexibility of being adapted and put on different stages for different audiences.

In this unit we focus on three novel-based movies: they are the masterpieces of three distinguished writers in the UK or US. *Pride and Prejudice* reflects the delicate relationship between wealth, status and marriage; *Gone with the Wind* unfolds before us the growing-up of a young pretty woman Scarlet as well as her love stories during the Civil War and the Reconstruction period; *For Whom the Bell Tolls* is about a young man's choice and dedication.

Unit Goals

- To have a general view of British and American literature;
- To know more about some famous writers and their works;
- To tell the discrepancies between the literature works and movies.

Unit Eight Literature

Section A Pride and Prejudice

> It is a truth universally acknowledged that a single man in possession of a good fortune must be in want of a wife.
> —Jane Austen in *Pride and Prejudice*

 I. Warm-up Questions

1. Can you name a few British writers or playwrights?
2. What British literature works do you know?
3. Who is Jane Austen? What are some of her masterpieces?

 II. Basics about the Movie

Genre: Romance
Director: Joe Wright
Starring: Keira Knightley
　　　　　Matthew Macfadyen
Release Year: 2005
Running Time: 127 minutes
Country: France, the United Kingdom, the United States

 III. Synopsis

Pride and Prejudice (2005) tells stories happening in the late 18th century in Britain. The Bennet couples together with their five daughters—Jane, Elizabeth, Mary, Kitty and Lydia—live in comparative financial independence as gentry at Longbourn, a working farm in rural England. According to the law of the time, the Bennet couples do not have a male inheritor, so Longbourn is destined to be inherited by Mr. Bennet's cousin, Mr. Collins.

It is imperative that Mrs. Bennet find proper husbands for her five daughters.

The arrival of a wealthy bachelor Charles Bingley causes a stir in the countryside, and the local families spare no efforts to introduce their daughters to the bachelor, with no exception of the Bonnets. Bingley falls in love with Jane at the first sight and a favorable marriage is supposed to be counted on. Unexpectedly, Bingley leaves without saying goodbye to Jane and Jane is heart-broken.

Mr. Darcy, Bingley's good friend, on the other hand, seems hard to please. He knits his brows and refuses to dance with ladies at the ball, which leaves a terrible impression on the mind of proud Elizabeth. Darcy's comment on Elizabeth's appearance further irritates her; they have varied opinions on some other issues. Mr. Darcy is attracted by Elizabeth's original ideas and struggles with her humble origin and eventually he plucks up courage but chooses an improper occasion to confess his love to her. It turns out that he is rejected in a blunt way with harsh words, which is also the climax and highlight of the whole film. Will Darcy put down his arrogance and pride? Will Elizabeth eliminate her prejudice and accept Darcy's love?

Ⅳ. Culture Links

1. A Brief Review of British Literature

On mentioning British literature, some names cannot be missed, such as **William Shakespeare**(威廉·莎士比亚,1564—1616), the greatest of all dramatists. His plays fall into three categories—comedy, tragedy and historical play, and have been put on in various forms on different stages. **George Bernard Shaw**(乔治·伯纳·萧,1856—1950) is said to be the greatest dramatist after Shakespeare.

A sequence of novelists and their works are also splendid treasures of British literature, such as **John Milton**'s *Paradise Lost*(《失乐园》) and *Paradise Regained*(《复乐园》), **Jonathan Swift**'s *Gulliver's Travels*(《格列佛游记》), and **Daniel Defoe**'s *Robinson Crusoe*(《鲁滨孙漂流记》). Besides, novelist **Charles Dickens** and his novels such as *Oliver Twist*(《雾都孤儿》), *Great Expectations*(《远大前程》), *A Tale of Two Cities*(《双城记》) and *David Copperfield*(《大卫·科波菲尔》) also go down with the history. **Thomas Hardy**(托马斯·哈代,1840—1928) and **Henry James**(亨利·詹姆斯,1843—1916) are two 20th-century distinguished novelists.

Geoffrey Chaucer(乔叟,1343—1400), the father of English literature, is widely considered the greatest English poet of the Middle Ages. He is best known today for *The*

Canterbury Tales(《坎特伯雷故事集》). There are also a galaxy of great poets in Britain, and most of them are born in the late 1800s and their poems thrive in the early 1900s, such as **Robert Burns**(罗伯特·彭斯,1759—1796), **William Wordsworth**(威廉·华兹华斯, 1770—1850), **Sir Walter Scott**(沃尔特·斯科特,1771—1832), **George Gordon Byron**(乔治·戈登·拜伦,1788—1824), **John Keats**(约翰·济慈,1795—1821), **Percy Bysshe Shelley**(波西·比希·雪莱,1792—1822). The period between 1798 and 1832 is called English Romanticism in literature. **William Butler Yeats**(威廉·帕特勒·叶芝,1865—1939) and **Thomas Stearns Eliot**(托马斯·斯特尔那斯·艾略特,1888—1965) are the outstanding representatives of modern poets.

What's worth special mentioning of the British literature is its contribution of talented female writers to the world literature. **Jane Austen**(简·奥斯汀,1775—1818) is one of the pioneer writers of Realistic Novel and she is good at using "irony". Her novels are called "Novel of Manners". The legendary Brontë Sisters are another pride of English literature. The Brontë Sisters were all highly talented but died young; their productions are acknowledged as masterpieces of literature: **Charlotte Brontë**'s (夏洛蒂·勃朗特,1816—1855) *Jane Eyre*(《简·爱》), **Emily Brontë**'s (艾米丽·勃朗特,1818—1848) *Wuthering Heights*(《呼啸山庄》) and **Anne Brontë**'s (安·勃朗特,1820—1849) *The Tenant of Wildfell House*(《王德弗尔大厅的房客》). **Virginia Woolf**(弗吉尼亚·伍尔夫,1882—1941) is a novelist and critic. Her novels are labeled as "stream of consciousness"(意识流). The United Kingdom's best-selling living author is also a female writer—**Joanne Rowling** who writes the *Harry Potter*(《哈利·波特》) fantasy series under the pen name J. K. Rowling. The *Harry Potter* series have been sold for more than 400 million copies.

2. Jane Austen (1775—1817)

Jane Austen, an English novelist, was born in Steventon, Hampshire, on 16 December 1775 and she lived there till her father retired from his priest position around 1800. Jane received little former education; she was mostly home educated by her father and brothers. Steventon witnessed Jane's encounter with the man of her dreams, Tom Lefroy in 1795 and her heartbroken in 1796. Her birthplace also saw the  writer's productivity from 1796 to 1799, during which period two of her best known novels *Sense and Sensibility*(《理智与情感》) and *Pride and Prejudice*(《傲慢与偏见》) were created and the latter was published under the title of *First Impression*.

After moving to Bath, the writer made revisions of her earlier novels and it was in Bath that she accepted a proposal which was to her great benefit and refused it the next morning.

The sudden death of Father in 1804 compelled the family to move to Southampton. Once again in 1809 the family chose to settle down in a new dwelling place, Chawton, a quiet cottage where the writer spent 8 years. She remained single all her life and died in 1817 at the age of 42.

Nowadays, Jane Austen's fans all over the world can commemorate the great writer at **Jane Austen Center**, a permanent exhibition to display the effect of visiting and living in Bath on the writing of the writer. Since 2000, the Jane Austen Festival has been annually celebrated in September in the town, which usually lasts for 9 days. The celebrations include Grand Regency Costumed Promenade(摄政盛装漫步), Walk Tour, Musical, etc.

Another museum for Jane Austen is located in Chawton, Hampshire, about 10 miles away from her birthplace. **Jane Austen's House Museum** is the only house where Jane lived and wrote open to the public. It is an independent museum established in 1947. July 18 of 2017 is the 200th anniversary of Jane Austen's death and a portrait of the writer appears on the 10-pound note, which on the other hand highlights her irreplaceable status in English literature.

* * *

Jane Austen is one of the most widely read writers in English literature and her popularity with the readers is only next to Shakespeare. As poet Alfred Tennyson put it, "Miss Austen understood the smallness of life to perfection. She was a great artist, equal in her small sphere to Shakespeare."

As an English novelist, she is known primarily for her six major novels, which interpret, critique and comment upon the British landed gentry in the end of the 18th century. Austen's plots often explore the dependence of women on marriage in the pursuit of favourable social standing and economic security. Her works critique the novels of sensibility of the second half of the 18th century and are part of the transition to 19th-century literary realism.

With the publications of *Sense and Sensibility*(1811), *Pride and Prejudice*(1813), *Mansfield Park*(《曼斯菲尔德庄园》,1814) and *Emma*(《爱玛》,1815), Jane Austen achieved success as a published writer. She wrote two additional novels, *Northanger Abbey* (《诺桑觉寺》) and *Persuasion*(《劝导》), both published posthumously in 1818, and began another, eventually titled *Sanditon*(《桑底顿》), but died before its completion. Her novels have rarely been out of print, although they were published anonymously and brought her little fame during her lifetime. A significant transition in her posthumous reputation occurred in 1869, fifty-two years after her death, when her nephew's publication of *A Memoir of Jane Austen*(《简·奥斯汀回忆录》) introduced her to a wider audience.

Jane Austen's use of biting irony, along with her realism and social commentary has earned her great and historical importance to critics and scholars.

* * *

Austen's novels have inspired the creation of many films, all her six well-known novels having been adapted into movies or TV series. At a rough estimate, *Pride and Prejudice* has been adapted for at least 10 times, ranging from its earliest adaption in 1938 and the latest in 2005. Some are Hollywood's productions and some are BBC's. Some are movies while some others are TV series. The latest movie *Love & Friendship* (2016) is adapted from Jane Austen's short epistolary novel *Lady Susan*(《苏珊夫人》).

Besides novel-based films, the writer's life experience, especially her love affair with Tom Lefroy has also been made into movies *Becoming Jane* (2007) and *Miss Austen's Regrets* (2008). A 2007 movie entitled *The Jane Austen Book Club* artfully integrates modern people's love and Jane Austen's novels within 106 minutes.

Ⅴ. Exercises

Multiple Choices: *Choose the best answer from the four choices given.*

1. *Pride and Prejudice* (2005) is a costume movie produced in the following three countries except _____.
   A. the UK   B. Ireland   C. the USA   D. France
2. The novel *Pride and Prejudice* was first published under the title of _____.
   A. First Encounter   B. First Impression

C. *Lady Susan*   D. *Little Woman*

3. According to the movie, which of the following is NOT true?

   A. Bingley falls in love with Jane Bonnet at the first sight.

   B. Collins is the inheritor of the Longbourn after the death of Mr. Bonnet.

   C. Darcy doesn't get along well with Vickham but finally they become brothers-in-law.

   D. Mrs. Bonnet spoils Lydia while Mary is the favorite of Mr. Bonnet.

4. Which of the following is not a British poet?

   A. William Wordsworth.   B. W. B. Yeats.

   C. Walt Whitman.   D. Alfred Tennyson.

5. Which of the following is a tragedy of Shakespeare?

   A. *A Midsummer Night's Dream*.   B. *Romeo and Juliet*.

   C. *As You Like It*.   D. *Much Ado About Nothing*.

6. Which of the following statements is NOT true about Jane Austen?

   A. She spent her whole life in British villages and towns.

   B. She received little schooling.

   C. She remained single all her life though she wrote so many romantic stories.

   D. She and her elder sister Cassandra Austen are both writers.

Blank-filling: *Fill in the blanks with the missing information.*

1. Jane Austen is famous for her six novels—they are _____, *Northanger Abbey*, _____, *Persuasion*, _____ and *Mansfield Park*.

2. The 19th-century Britain abounds in poets, of which _____, Samuel Taylor Coleridge and _____ are called the Lake Poets because they all lived in the lake districts.

3. William Shakespeare is unequalled in terms of his productivity, versatility and the influence on the world literature. As a poet, he created 154 _____; as a playwright, he first wrote many _____ such as *Henry IV* and *Richard III*, _____ such as *The Twelfth Night* and *The Merchant of Venice* as well as _____ such as *Hamlet* and *King Lear*.

4. _____ is reputed as the father of English literature, whose representative work is _____.

5. In British literature, there are several important female novelists including the most wide read writer _____, the legendary family _____, George Eliot, and _____.

Unit Eight Literature

➤ **Appreciate & Dub**: *Watch the video clip again to appreciate how Darcy confesses his feelings to Elizabeth. Then try to dub the climax of the movie.*

Darcy: (*cont'd*) I came to Rosings with the single object of seeing you... I had to see you.

Lizzie: Me?

Darcy: I've fought against my better judgment, my family's expectation...

(pause)

Darcy: (*cont'd*) The inferiority of your birth...my rank and circumstance... (*stumblingly*) all those things... but I'm willing to put them aside... and ask you to end my agony...

Lizzie: I don't understand...

Darcy: (*with passion*) I love you. Most ardently.

Lizzie stares at him.

Darcy: (*cont'd*) Please do me the honour of accepting my hand.

A silence. Lizzie struggles with the most painful confusion of feeling. Finally she recovers.

Lizzie: (*voice shaking*) Sir, I appreciate the struggle you have been through, and I am very sorry to have caused you pain. Believe me, it was unconsciously done.

A silence. Gathering her shawl, she gets to her feet.

Darcy: (*stares*) Is this your reply?

Lizzie: Yes, sir.

Darcy: Are you laughing at me?

Lizzie: No!

Darcy: Are you rejecting me?

Lizzie: (*pause*) I'm sure that the feelings which, as you've told me, have hindered your regard, will help you in overcoming it.

A terrible silence, as this sinks in. Neither of them can move. At last, Darcy speaks. He is very pale.

Darcy: Might I ask why, with so little endeavour at civility, I am thus repulsed?

Lizzie: (*trembling with emotion*) I might as well enquire why, with so evident a design of insulting me, you chose to tell me that you liked me against your better judgment. If I was uncivil, that was some excuse—

Darcy: Believe me, I didn't mean.

Lizzie: But I have other reasons, you know I have!

Darcy: What reasons?

Lizzie: Do you think that anything might tempt me to accept the man who has ruined, perhaps for ever, the happiness of a most beloved sister?

Silence. Darcy looks as if he's been struck across the face.

Lizzie: (*cont'd*) Do you deny it, Mr. Darcy, that you've separated a young couple who loved each other, exposing your friend to the censure of the world for caprice, and my sister to its derision for disappointed hopes, and involving them both in misery of the acutest kind?

Darcy: I do not deny it.

Lizzie: (*blurts out*) How could you do it?

Darcy: Because I believed your sister indifferent to him.

Lizzie: Indifferent.

Darcy: I watched them most carefully, and realized his attachment was much deeper than hers.

Lizzie: That's because she's shy!

Darcy: Bingley too is modest, and was persuaded that she didn't feel strongly for him.

Lizzie: Because you suggested it!

Darcy: I did it for his own good.

Lizzie: My sister hardly shows her true feelings to me! (*pause, takes a breath*) I suppose you suspect that his fortune had same bearing on the matter?

Darcy: (*sharply*) No! I wouldn't do your sister the dishonour. Though it was suggested. (*stops*)

Lizzie: What was?

Darcy: It was made perfectly clear that... an advantageous marriage... (*stops*)

Lizzie: Did my sister give that impression?

Darcy: No!

An awkward pause.

Darcy: (*cont'd*) There was, however, I have to admit... the matter of your family.

Lizzie: Our want of connection? Mr Bingley didn't vex himself about that!

Darcy: No, it was more than that.

Lizzie: How, sir?

Darcy: (*pause, very uncomfortable*) It pains me to say this, but it was the lack of propriety shown by your mother, your three younger sisters even, on occasion, your father. Forgive me.

Lizzie blushes. He has hit home. Darcy paces up and down.

Unit Eight   Literature

Darcy: (*cont'd*) You and your sister I must exclude from this…
Darcy stops. He is in turmoil. Lizzie glares at him, ablaze.

VI. Critical Thinking

1. In *Pride and Prejudice* (2005), there are five couples and different types of marriages. Are there any differences in the essence of their marriage? How do you comment their marriages?

2. Mrs. Bonnet, who is readily to marry her daughters off to wealthy bachelors, sometimes at the cost of her dignity, resembles the image of mother-in-law in some China's TV series. How do you like Mrs. Bonnet?

Section B Gone with the Wind

> After all, tomorrow is another day!
>
> —Scarlett in *Gone with the Wind*

 I. Warm-up Questions

1. What is your favourite romance movie?
2. Do you know any American writers or poets?
3. Clark Gable and Vivien Leigh are long regarded as one of the classical screen lovers. Do you know any other such screen lovers?

 II. Basics about the Movie

Genre: epic, history, romance
Director: Victor Fleming
Starring: Clark Gable, Vivien Leigh, Leslie Howard, Olivia de Havilland
Release Year: 1939
Running Time: 221 minutes
Country: the United States

 III. Synopsis

Gone with the Wind is a two-part film shot in 1939, lasting for 3 hours and 41 minutes. The movie was adapted from Margaret Mitchell's 1936 novel of the same name. The leading roles were played by the Hollywood's stars Vivien Leigh and Clark Gable.

This tale begins from the Civil War of the US. Scarlett O'Hara, the most beautiful girl of the town, at the O'Hara plantation, Tara, could only be described as genteel. She is always the belle of the ball and eager to win him over, Ashley Wilkes. At the barbecue at the nearby Wilkes plantation, she is dismayed to hear that Ashley is to marry his cousin Melanie Hamilton and in a fit of anger, she decides to marry Melanie's brother. At the Twelfth Oak plantation, Scarlett first meets Rhett Butler, a dropout from the West Point and black sheep from the Charleston.

War is soon declared and men march off to battle. In the war the newly-married Scarlett becomes a widow. When she travels to Atlanta, Scarlett sees the ravages that war brings. She also becomes re-acquainted with Rhett Butler. Still, she pines for married Ashley and dreams of his return. When she returns to Tara and faces the hardship of surviving her family, she becomes hardened and bitter and will do anything, even marrying her sister's beau to ensure she will never again be poor and hungry. But she becomes a widow for the second time.

Rhett Butler, who always comes to Scarlett's rescue during her hardships, finally proposes to her. Rhett spoils Scarlett and their daughter in every means. But they soon find themselves working at cross-purposes, because Scarlett still hangs on Ashley. After their daughter Bonnie's death incidentally, the relationship of Scarlett and Rhett seems doomed from the outset.

Ⅳ. Culture Links

1. A Brief Review of American Literature

American literature can be traced back to the 15th-century European exploration writings. Since then many schools of literature have emerged from the new continent, such as the Romanticism, the Realism, the Naturalism and the Modernism.

Many great writers and poets sprang up from the rich soil such as **Ralph Waldo Emerson**(拉尔夫·沃尔多·爱默生,1803—1882), **Henry David Thoreau**(亨利·戴维·梭罗,1817—1862), **Herman Melville**(赫尔曼·梅尔维尔,1819—1891), **Theodore Dreiser**(西奥多·德莱塞,1871—1945), **Jack London**(杰克·伦敦,1876—1916), **John Steinbeck**(约翰·斯坦贝克,1902—1968). **The Lost Generation** was prevalent in the middle of the 20th-century American literature. **The Beat Generation** was represented by **Jack Kerouac**(杰克·凯鲁亚克,1922—1969) and his *On the Road*(《在路上》,1957).

The masterpiece of Theodore Dreiser is *An American Tragedy*(《美国悲剧》,1965), for which the writer is acclaimed as the greatest novelist in American history. Jack London's *Martin Eden* (《马丁·伊登》,1909), John Steinbeck's *The Grapes of Wrath*(《愤怒的葡

萄》,1939), **Joseph Heller**'s(约瑟夫·海勒,1923—1999) *Catch-22*(《第二十二条军规》,1961) are permanent classics in American Literature.

2. Margaret Mitchell(玛格丽特·米切尔,1900—1949)

Margaret Mitchell had only one novel published during her life time—*Gone with the Wind*, which won her two honors: the National Book Award for Most Distinguished Novel of 1936 and the Pulitzer Prize for Fiction in 1937. It was adapted into a 1939 American film. *Gone with the Wind* was popular with American readers from the outset and was the top American fiction bestseller in the year when it was published and in 1937. As of 2014, a Harris poll found it to be the second favorite book of American readers, just behind the Bible. More than 30 million copies have been printed worldwide.

Margaret Mitchell was a Southerner and a lifelong resident and native of Atlanta, Georgia. She was born in 1900 into a wealthy and politically prominent family. She used to be a reporter and began to write novels with the support of her husband. She was praised for her imaginative use of color in the novel, especially the colors red and green, which surround Scarlett O'Hara.

3. American Slavery

Slavery in the United States was the legal institution of human chattel enslavement, primarily of Africans and African Americans. It existed in the United States of America in the 18th and 19th centuries after the USA gained its independence and before the end of the American Civil War. Slavery had been practiced in British America from early colonial days, and was legal in all Thirteen Colonies at the time when *The Declaration of Independence* was issued in 1776.

By the time of the American Revolution (1775—1783), the status of slave had been institutionalized as a racial caste associated with African ancestry. When the United States Constitution was ratified (1789), a relatively small number of free people of color were among the voting citizens (male property owners). During and immediately following the Revolutionary War, abolitionist laws were passed in most Northern states and a movement developed to abolish slavery. Most of these states had a higher proportion of free labor than in the South and economies based on different industries. They abolished slavery by the end of the 18th century, some with gradual systems that kept adults as slaves for two decades. But the rapid expansion of the cotton industry in the Deep South after the invention of the cotton gin greatly increased demand for slave labor, and the Southern states continued as slave societies. Those states attempted to extend slavery into the new Western territories to keep their share of political power in the nation; Southern leaders also wanted to annex Cuba to be used as a slave territory. The United States became polarized over the issue of slavery, represented by the slave and free states divided by the Mason—Dixon line, which separated free Pennsylvania from slave Maryland and Delaware.

Congress during the Jefferson's administration prohibited the importation of slaves, effective in 1808, although smuggling(走私) was not unusual. Domestic slave trading, however, continued at a rapid pace, driven by labor demands from the development of cotton plantations in the Deep South. More than one million slaves were sold from the Upper South, which had a surplus of labor, and taken to the Deep South in a forced migration, splitting up many families. New communities of African-American culture were developed in the Deep South, and the total slave population in the South eventually reached 4 million before liberation.

As the West was developed for settlement, the Southern state governments wanted to keep a balance between the number of slaves and free states to maintain a political balance of power in Congress. The new territories acquired from Britain, France, and Mexico were the subject of major political compromises. By 1850, the newly rich cotton-growing South was threatening to secede from the Union, and tensions continued to rise. Many white Southern Christians, including church ministers, attempted to justify their support for slavery as modified by Christian paternalism(家长式制度).

When Abraham Lincoln won the 1860 election on a platform of halting the expansion of slavery, seven states broke away to form the Confederacy. The first six states to secede held the greatest number of slaves in the South. Shortly after, the Civil War began when Confederate forces attacked the US Army's Fort Sumter. Four additional slave states then seceded. Due to Union measures such as the *Confiscation Acts* and *Emancipation Proclamation* in 1863, the war effectively ended slavery, even before ratification of the *Thirteenth Amendment* in December 1865 formally ended the legal institution throughout the United States.

Anglo-American Classic Movies and Culture

 Ⅴ. **Exercises**

➤ **True or False Statements**: *Read the following statements and decide whether they are true (T) or false (F).*

_____1. *Gone with the Wind*, one of the best known novels of Margaret Mitchell, was made into an Oscar-winning movie in 1939.

_____2. The social background of *Gone with the Wind* was the American Civil War, when America was still the colony of Great Britain.

_____3. Before the American Civil War, the Northern states were opposed to slavery and their principal aim of the war was to defeat the forces of Confederate and made America a united country.

_____4. Around the American Civil War, the Industrial Revolution had not happened in America.

_____5. Rhett Butler didn't think there was much likelihood for the Confederacy to win the war so he refused to join the army.

_____6. Scarlett fell in love with Melanie's brother after she got the heart-broken news that Ashley was engaged to Melanie.

_____7. The tide of war turned against the Confederacy after the Battle of Gettysburg in which many of the men of Scarlett's town were killed.

_____8. Scarlett married Rhett Butler after the death of her second husband, but she still had affection for Ashley.

_____9. After the American Civil War, slavery was not abolished in the United States of America.

_____10. At the end of the story Rhett Butler felt disappointed and he was determined to leave Scarlett.

➤ **Short-answer Questions**: *Give brief answers to the following questions.*

1. When was American slavery abolished?

   _____

   _____

   _____

Unit Eight Literature

2. Can you name three American novelists and their representative works?

   _____
   _____
   _____
   _____

3. What are some of the schools of literature in American history? List at least four.

   _____
   _____
   _____
   _____

◆ **Extracurricular Exploration**: *Explore the Internet. Find out the answers to the following questions and make a no-more-than-5-minute presentation.*

   1. Tell the background of the story of *Gone with the Wind*.

   2. Pick out one of the renowned American writers and introduce the writer and his/her works to the class.

   3. Can you continue the story and share with your classmates what happens later?

Section C　For Whom the Bell Tolls

Ⅰ. Movie Information (Explore and Find)

Genre: _____
Chinese Title: _____
Director: _____
Starring: _____
Running Time: _____ minutes
Release Year: 1943
Country: _____

➤ Use the information you have found to fill in the blanks.

For Whom the Bell Tolls is a _____ (year) _____ (country) _____ (genre) film inspired by the story of _____ from the Book of _____. The film stars _____ as Robert Jordan, along with Ingrid Bergman, Akim Tamiroff, etc. The story is mainly about _____ life _____ around _____, fighting against fascism as well as his _____. The film ends with Jordan firing the Lewis gun directly at the camera.

Ⅱ. Synopsis

During the Spanish Civil War, an American language teacher, Robert Jordan, who lived in Spain during the pre-war period, fights in the International Brigades against Francisco Franco's forces. As an experienced dynamiter, Jordan is sent on a mission of destroying a critical bridge with the aid of a band of local anti-fascist guerrillas(游击队员). The bridge must be blown up to prevent enemy troops from travelling across it to respond to an upcoming offensive against the fascists.

Jordan meets an old guerrilla fighter, Anselmo, who helps Jordan establish relationship with a group of Republican guerrillas under the leadership of Pablo. Jordan falls in love with one guerrilla named María, whose life was shattered by her parents' execution and her gang-rape at the hands of the Falangists (part of the fascist coalition) at the outbreak of the war. Jordan has a strong sense of duty, which clashes with the unwillingness of Pablo to commit to helping with the bridge-blowing operation. At the same time, Jordan develops a new-found lust for life which arises from his love for María. Pablo's wife, Pilar, usurps(篡夺) Pablo's leadership and pledges the allegiance of the guerrillas to Jordan's mission. However, when another band of anti-fascist guerrillas, led by El Sordo, are surrounded and killed in a desperate last stand, Pablo destroys Jordan's dynamite detonation equipment (炸药爆炸装置), hoping to prevent the bridge demolition and thereby avoid fascist reprisals on his camp. Later, Pablo regrets abandoning his comrades and returns to assist in the operation.

However, the enemies, apprised of the coming offensive, have prepared to ambush the Republicans in force and it seems unlikely that blowing up the bridge will do much to prevent a rout. Regardless, Jordan understands that he must still demolish the bridge in an attempt to prevent fascist reinforcements from overwhelming his allies. Lacking the equipment destroyed by Pablo, Jordan and Anselmo improvise a more dangerous alternative method to explode the dynamite by using hand grenades.

While the guerrilla fighters—Pablo, Pilar, and María—create a diversion for Jordan and Anselmo, the two men plant and detonate the dynamite, costing Anselmo his life when he is hit by a piece of debris from the exploding bridge. While the guerrillas are escaping on horseback, Jordan is maimed when a fascist tank shoots his horse out from under him. Jordan is shot and he doesn't want his comrades to be endangered. He bids goodbye to María, armed with a Lewis machine gun. He waits, fires a sweeping barrage at the oncoming soldiers and sacrifices his life.

III. Culture Links

1. Ernest Miller Hemingway (1899—1961)

Ernest Miller Hemingway was an American novelist, short-story writer, and journalist. His economical and understated style had a strong influence on the 20th-century fiction, while his life of adventure and his public image influenced later generations.

He participated in World War I as an ambulance driver and was seriously wounded; he served as a war-time journalist in the Spanish Civil War; he was in China as a commissioner in 1941 when China

was fighting with the invading Japanese; he also witnessed Normandy landings and the liberation of Paris during World War Ⅱ. Many of his war-time experiences turned to be basis of his upcoming novels such as *A Farewell to Arms* (1929) and *For Whom the Bell Tolls* (1940). In 1954, while in Africa, Hemingway was almost fatally injured in two successive plane crashes and his health was seriously damaged.

Hemingway produced most of his works between the mid-1920s and the mid-1950s, and won the Nobel Prize in Literature in 1954. His other works such as *The Sun Also Rises* (1926) and *The Old Man and the Sea* (1952) are also considered classics of American literature. He killed himself in the mid-1962.

2. Spanish Civil War (1936—1939)

The Spanish Civil War took place from 1936 to 1939, or simply as the Civil War in Spain. The Republicans, who were loyal to the democratic, left-leaning and relatively urban Second Spanish Republic, in an alliance of convenience with the Anarchists, fought against the Nationalists, a Falangist, Carlist, and largely aristocratic conservative group led by General Francisco Franco. Although the war is often portrayed as a struggle between democracy and fascism, some historians believe it should more accurately be described as a struggle between leftist revolution and rightist counter-revolution. Ultimately, the Nationalists won, and Franco then ruled Spain for the next 36 years, from April 1939 until his death in November 1975.

3. Fascism

Fascism is a form of radical authoritarian nationalism, characterized by dictatorial power, forcible suppression of opposition and control of industry and commerce that came to prominence in early 20th-century Europe. The first fascist movements emerged in Italy during World War Ⅰ before it spread to other European countries.

Since the end of World War Ⅱ in 1945, few parties have openly described themselves as fascist and the term is instead now usually used pejoratively by political opponents. The descriptions neo-fascist or post-fascist are sometimes applied more formally to describe parties of the far-right with ideologies similar to, or rooted in, 20th-century fascist movements.

Unit Eight Literature

 IV. Expansion

In the 20th-century American literature history, there are two literature schools, which are respectively labeled as the Lost Generation and the Beat Generation. Make a comparison of the two schools.

	The Lost Generation	The Beat Generation
Origin of the name		
Active years		
Leader of each school		
Representative works		
Theme of the works		
Influence		

 V. Fun Time

For Whom the Bell Tolls (1943) tells us that during the Spanish Civil War, an American allied with the Republicans finds romance during a desperate mission to blow up a strategically important bridge. On the contrary, the film *The Bridge on the River Kwai* (1957) depicts a group of British soldiers and colonels who are taken prisoners by the Japanese and are arranged to build a bridge. Look at the following video clips from *The Bridge on the River Kwai* (1957) and summarize the main idea of the part.

Theme: _____

Key points: _____

_____

_____

_____

_____

Appendix

Kings and Queens Since 1066

Timeline of the Kings and Queens of England from 1066 to 1603	
The Normans （诺曼王朝） (1066—1154)	
Plantagenets （金雀花王朝） (1154—1399)	
The House of Lancaster （兰卡斯特王朝） (1399—1461)	The House of York （约克王朝） (1461—1485)
The Tudors （都铎王朝） (1485—1603)	

续表

Kings and Queens of the United Kingdom from 1603 to the present day
The Stuarts* 　（斯图亚特王朝） 　（1603—1649）（1660—1714）
The House of Hanover 　（汉诺威王朝） 　（1714—1901）
Saxe-Coburg-Gotha　　　and The Windsors 　（萨克森—科堡—哥达王朝）　（温莎王朝） 　（1901—1910）　　　　　　（1917—Today）

* During the time between 1649 and 1660, there was no King or Queen in Britain when the country was a republic between 1649 and 1660. In 1649 King Charles Ⅰ was executed and Britain became a Republic for eleven years. The monarchy was restored in 1660.

Kings and Queens Since 1066

The Normans（1066—1154）
- King William Ⅰ（the Conqueror）1066—1087[①]
- King William Ⅱ（Rufus）1087—1100
- King Henry Ⅰ 1100—1135
- King Stephen 1135—1154
- Empress Matilda 1141

The House of Amjou（Plantagenet）（1154—1399）
- King Henry Ⅱ 1154—1189
- King Richard Ⅰ（the Lionheart）1189—1199
- King John Ⅰ 1199—1216
- King Henry Ⅲ 1216—1272
- King Edward Ⅰ 1272—1307
- King Edward Ⅱ 1307—1327
- King Edward Ⅲ 1327—1377
- Richard Ⅱ 1377—1399

The House of Lancaster（1399—1461）
- Henry Ⅳ 1399—1413
- Henry Ⅴ 1413—1422
- Henry Ⅵ 1422—1461，1470—1471

The House of York（1461—1485）
- King Edward Ⅳ 1461—1470，1471—1483
- King Edward Ⅴ 1483
- King Richard Ⅲ 1483—1485

The Tudors（1485—1603）
- King Henry Ⅶ 1485—1509
- King Henry Ⅷ 1509—1547

---

① 所列时间均为在位时间。

- King Edward VI 1547—1553
- Jane Grey 1553
- Queen Mary I (Bloody Mary) 1553—1558
- Queen Elizabeth I 1558—1603

The Stuarts (1603—1649)(1660—1714)

- James I 1603—1625
- Charles I 1625—1649
- Charles II 1660—1685
- James II 1685—1688
- William III 1689—1702 and Queen Mary II 1689—1694
- Queen Anne 1702—1714

The House of Hanover (1714—1901)

- King George I 1714—1727
- King George II 1727—1760
- King George III 1760—1820
- King George IV 1820—1830
- King William IV 1830—1837
- Queen Victoria 1837—1901

Saxe-Coburg-Gotha (1901—1910) and **The Windsors** (1917—Today)

- King Edward VII 1901—1910
- King George V 1910—1936
- King Edward VIII 1936
- King George VI 1936—1952
- Queen Elizabeth II 1952—present day

主要参考书目

［1］黄奕,马琼.美国文化探奇:风俗背后的故事［M］.西安:西安交通大学出版社,1999.

［2］王恩铭.美国文化与社会［M］.上海:上海外语教育出版社,2009.

［3］刘华,徐亮,陈立.英文电影赏析［M］.上海:上海交通大学出版社,2014.

［4］Andrew Lynn.英语电影赏析［M］.霍斯亮,译.北京:外语教学与研究出版社,2005.

［5］刘春伟.英语国家人文知识概况［M］.北京:机械工业出版社,2008.

［6］金利.跟随电影看英国［M］.北京:科学出版社,2013.

［7］黄际英,侯丹,王丽娟.博学英语·英美影视欣赏［M］.上海:复旦大学出版社,2006.

［8］谢福之.英语国家概况［M］.北京:外语教学与研究出版社,2013.

［9］Maxine F. Huffman, Donald M. Huffman.走进美国文化［M］.北京:外语教学与研究出版社,2009.

［10］http://www.imdb.com

［11］http://www.metacritic.com

［13］http://www.wikipedia.com

［14］http://www.listeningexpress.com/englishmovies/dialogues/